Irish Sociological Chron
volume 4 (2001–

PLACE AND NON-PLACE

THE RECONFIGURATION OF IRELAND

Edited by Michel Peillon and Mary P. Corcoran

IPA
INSTITUTE OF PUBLIC
ADMINISTRATION

First Published 2004
by the Institute of Public Administration
57-61 Lansdowne Road
Dublin 4
Ireland

Many of the images in this publication were selected by Alexa Coyne, Visual Arts Programmer of the Civil Arts Inquiry. The purpose of the Civil Arts Inquiry is, firstly, to make a series of propositions about the future identity and role of the City Arts Centre and secondly, about the role of culture and arts in Ireland and in society in general.

ISBN 1-904541-06-2
ISSN 1393-7464

British Library Cataloguing in Publication Data
A catalogue record for this book is available from the British Library

Cover image by Conor Caffrey, Greystones, Co. Wicklow
Cover design by M. and J. Graphics Ltd, Dublin
Typeset in 10.75/13 New Century Schoolbook
by Computertype Ltd, Dublin
Printed in Ireland by ColourBooks Ltd, Dublin

Contents

	Contributors	vii
	Preface	ix
INTRODUCTION		
1	Introduction: The reconfiguration of Ireland *Michel Peillon and Mary P. Corcoran*	1
PART 1: MARKET SOCIETY?		
2	Falling over the competitive edge *Seán Ó Riain*	19
3	Social capital and regional growth *Amanda Haynes*	30
4	The "gift" relation and Irish consumerism *Kieran Keohane and Carmen Kuhling*	43
5	Selling soccer *Mark O'Brien*	54
6	Denizens and citizens *Bryan Fanning*	65
PART 2: DISPLACED REPRESENTATIONS		
7	The relics of St Thérèse *Richard O'Leary*	83
8	Digging up the past *Farrel Corcoran*	93
9	Playing the second fiddle? Young men and masculinity in Northern Ireland *Dirk Schubotz and Bill Rolston*	103

10 Nature as artefact on Bull Island 111
Stephen Quilley

PART 3: GOING PLACES

11 Selling regional identity: The case of Fuchsia Brands Ltd 131
Ethel Crowley

12 Place re-making in Dublin 142
Mary P. Corcoran

13 Brandcentral 157
İ. Emre Işık

14 The making of the Dublin conurbation 167
Michel Peillon

PART 4: TENSIONS AND CONTRAVENTIONS

15 The land of conditional welcomes 185
Gerard W. Boucher

16 Cows in Dublin, public spaces and public transport 196
James Wickham

17 Random attacks? 206
Ciaran McCullagh

18 Reclaiming the streets 217
Joe Moffatt

Contributors

Gerard W. BOUCHER, Trinity College Dublin
Farrel CORCORAN, Dublin City University
Mary P. CORCORAN, National University of Ireland, Maynooth
Ethel CROWLEY, Trinity College Dublin
Bryan FANNING, University College Dublin
Amanda HAYNES, University of Limerick
İ. Emre IŞIK, National University of Ireland, Maynooth
Kieran KEOHANE, University College Cork
Carmen KUHLING, University of Limerick
Ciaran McCULLAGH, University College Cork
Joe MOFFATT, National University of Ireland, Maynooth
Mark O'BRIEN, Dublin City University
Richard O'LEARY, Queen's University, Belfast
Seán Ó RIAIN, National University of Ireland, Maynooth
Michel PEILLON, National University of Ireland, Maynooth
Stephen QUILLEY, University College Dublin
Bill ROLSTON, University of Ulster
Dirk SCHUBOTZ, University of Ulster
James WICKHAM, Trinity College Dublin

Preface

We are delighted to introduce the fourth volume in the *Irish Sociological Chronicles* series. In keeping with the style established in the earlier volumes, we have assembled a range of essays that are topical, accessible and somewhat shorter in length than the typical academic article.

There is an ongoing debate within the discipline as to whether and how sociology should adopt a more public role. A concern of many is that sociological writing is sometimes obtuse and somewhat removed from the social reality of everyday life. In other words, sociologists do not always present their views and insights in a manner that can be accessed and understood by the general public. Yet sociologists are engaged in the important task of monitoring the social world, interrogating the changes that are occurring, and interpreting the experiences of people as they navigate their way through life. The *Irish Sociological Chronicles* series seeks to make an intervention in the public sphere by providing a space in which sociologists can reflect in a sociologically relevant way on current matters that catch their imagination, and which we hope will catch the imagination of you, the reader. The series, therefore, provides an important outlet for sociologists seeking to bring their work and their insights into the wider public domain.

The first volume in this series was conceived as an invitation to both the general and specialist reader to engage with the project of sociology and to discover what sociologists have to say about Irish society. We believe that sociology continues to have something useful to say about the nature and direction of the changes occurring in Irish society, and that this series offers the reader a unique opportunity to interpret and reflect on those changes. The essays in this volume cover the years 2001 and 2002, a period during which the effects of the Celtic Tiger era, both direct and indirect, began to work their way through the fabric of Irish society. Post-industrialism has emerged as a dominant narrative to explain Irish development and many of the essays interrogate the mythological quality of this narrative and also the ways in which it interacts with and helps to structure other sectors of Irish society. The significance of place surfaces as a major theme in this collection. The contributors grapple with the way in which place – as a spatial and a symbolic construct – is being reconceptualised and reconfigured, producing in the process both displacement and non-places.

As with the previous volumes, this collection is the outcome of collaborative effort and we would like to thank a number of people for their contribution. When we approached Declan McGonagle – then at the City Arts Centre, now Chair of Arts and Design at the University of Ulster – to investigate the possibility of including the work of artists in the volume, he was not only positive but enthusiastic. Declan and his colleague Alexa Coyne helped us to assemble the images interspersed throughout the book, which offer their own commentary on place and non-place in Irish society. We are grateful to all the artists who allowed us to reproduce their work here. The Institute of Public Administration continues its support for the *Irish Sociological Chronicles*, and we want particularly to thank Jennifer Armstrong for her input. Our thanks also go to the contributors, without whom there would be no volume, and whose work provides a fascinating insight into the ongoing reconfiguration of Irish society.

CHAPTER 1

Introduction: The Reconfiguration of Ireland

MICHEL PEILLON AND MARY P. CORCORAN

Societies, like individuals, tell stories about themselves: about who they are and what they want to become. Or rather, various groups and individuals relate stories about society, and they do so for their own purpose and according to their own agenda. Many such tales will never enjoy wide acceptance, but some acquire plausibility and are widely upheld. It would be pointless to attempt to measure them against actual social reality. These stories are myths or crystallisations of meaning that offer a way of making sense of the surrounding social world and, as such, can only be related to other myths.

The history of Ireland is wrapped up in myths, some of which still enjoy considerable currency in various circles, for example the image of rural arcadia or the assertion of a distinctive Irish character. One of these myths has remained particularly potent and is endlessly narrated. It constitutes the founding myth of modern Ireland: after a long period of economic stagnation, T. K. Whitaker and Seán Lemass reversed the fortunes of Ireland by opening it to the wider world and creating the conditions of its industrialisation. That myth invariably acts as the touchstone for the stories that we generate about ourselves in twenty-first century Ireland.

A post-industrial narrative

Social scientists are no less inclined to produce such narratives, even if they claim for their stories a special status of truthfulness. The latest story that is being told about Ireland, and that Ireland is more and more telling about itself, is that it is on its way to becoming an information or, better still, a knowledge society. In brief, Ireland purports to have entered the rather exclusive circle of those advanced economies that boast the title of post-industrial. The contention that Ireland has become a knowledge society, however, stretches credibility. Ireland's particularly low level of investment in research and development, for instance, gives the lie to such a view. And the variable quality of infrastructure for electronic communication does not inspire much confidence in the country's informational future.

However, Ireland has carved itself a niche within global post-industrial capitalism. While this does not make the Irish economy a fully fledged post-industrial one, it nonetheless means that whatever economic growth has taken place has been to a great extent based on the post-industrial sector, and the ripple effects of that are felt throughout society. The emphasis on post-industrialism catches a crucial element of contemporary Ireland. But it does not tell the whole story; it does not provide an adequate context for understanding the powerful ways in which this new dynamic interacts with other sectors of society. This is where the story becomes a myth: sufficiently real to be plausible and make sense, but partial because of what it does not say.

The post-industrial sector forms itself as a niche within the Irish economy and society. Such a statement probably applies to most advanced economies, but its relevance in Ireland is enhanced by the fact that post-industrialism has been implanted from the outside. Not only that, but it has been implanted on a society that was hardly industrial. Ireland may not be the only country manifesting these features, but it represents a particularly significant case.

It offers an opportunity to understand how this dynamic of post-industrialism unfolds and how it impacts on the society that it penetrates. The story of these interactions acts as a counterweight to the prevailing myth of post-industrialism.

The volumes in the *Irish Sociological Chronicles* series contribute in various ways to building a narrative about Ireland. The first volume, *Encounters with Modern Ireland*, relates to the years 1995 and 1996, and looks at Ireland at a very special time in terms of its economic prosperity and the changing nature of society. The book records some of the processes involved in this transformation: an intensification of the process of commodification, chiefly in cultural terms; a more sustained dialectic of global and local forces; a greater emphasis on visual features; and in some respects a growing reflexivity, with suggestions of fragmentation.

The second volume, covering the years 1997 and 1998, follows these processes as they unfold and shape a new Ireland. *Memories of the Present* points to the growing confidence and sense of celebration that accompanied economic success, but it also highlights some of the problems generated by it. Identities are being renegotiated; reflexivity encounters resistance from various quarters; and global processes face local factors and forces.

The third volume in the series chronicles the turn from the twentieth to the twenty-first century. Even if economic prosperity could not be sustained, the transformation of Ireland was by then deep and irreversible. *Ireland Unbound* examines the shifting contours of Irish society and, in particular, the ways in which the boundaries that structure Irish society are being remodelled. Some have dissolved, some have proved resilient to change, and some have crossed over each other melding or producing uneasy interfaces.

Now, the lines along which Irish society is being re-organised are becoming sharper. *Place and Non-Place*, the fourth volume in the series, considers the way Irish society is being reconfigured. Although the term post-industrial has hardly been used, at least not in any significant way, the *Irish Sociological Chronicles* have been telling a story of Ireland becoming in some way, in its own way, post-industrial. This particular volume of chronicles examines how the growing post-industrial element within Ireland is interacting with and structuring Irish society as a whole.

Fault lines

Such a reconfiguration does not involve a smooth transformation. It activates a range of internal tensions and contradictions that come to form the fault lines along which Irish society is constructed and according to which, in a fundamental way, the society remains vulnerable to further structural changes. Some of these contradictions are highlighted in the contributions to this volume.

The foremost tension relates to the conditions under which Ireland can participate in a global economy. The global orientation of the Irish economy is in fact embedded in a local context and the most forward sectors of the economy thrive on existing personal and institutional networks. The partnership framework has also been identified as a major factor in the new economy of Ireland. In a sense, partnership represents the opposite of market relations: it requires that the relations between the major socio-economic players are not left to their own logic, but are instead regulated, constrained by norms that have been negotiated and agreed upon. The tension between the market and partnership programmes can be a creative one, but the balance between them remains precarious. For this reason, competitiveness may have little to do with the unfettered play of the market but be enhanced by links between firms and by sustained co-operation between economic agents.

This tension, and possibly contradiction, between the economic logic of the market and the requirements of solidarity finds other kinds of expression. Attempts to commercialise or cash in on national assets generate a certain disquiet. Similarly, there is much soul searching about the alleged materialism of Ireland. This consumerism derives in part from the market, with its logic of accumulation, but, more fundamentally, it follows a logic of reciprocity according to which the community is organised and sustained. The tension between the free play of market mechanisms and the effort at social inclusion has not been solved by the state in relation to immigration. This tension manifests itself as fragmentation within the state apparatus itself: between those state agencies that issue work permits to address skill shortages and those public agencies that are concerned with more general service provision for asylum seekers.

A fault line also extends across Irish public space. How public space is managed, developed and redeveloped is a matter of public contestation. The capacity to enter and use public space is circumscribed by the increasing levels of incivility in our society. The source of this incivility, or to be more precise the conditions that allow it to flourish, may be embedded deeply in our social institutions and public services. So despite the capacity to spin a story of the modern Irish as sophisticates who have come of age, in everyday social practice – particularly on the streets of cities and towns – that myth is continually contested.

A market society?

In the first part of this book, the case is made that the economic market, which is widely presented as the panacea for economic growth, is framed by a social context. This social context determines the extent to which market mechanisms effectively ensure economic development. Seán Ó Riain argues that, in the aftermath of the Celtic Tiger, the future success of the Irish economy depends on the development of a high-skill innovation-based economy. However, the competitiveness model supported by government and predicated on low wages and cost cutting seriously undermines the prospect of this. He stresses that market relations are rooted in communal relationships and institutions of solidarity, and these must be supported through public investment in order to achieve sustained economic development in Ireland.

Competitiveness is also the main consideration in Amanda Haynes's chapter. She looks at the National Spatial Strategy, the most recent expression of regional policy formulated by the government. Such a strategy focuses on agglomerations that enjoy a critical mass sufficient to sustain innovation and economic development. Drawing on a study of relations between information technology firms in Galway, Haynes contends that a balanced regional distribution of public and infrastructural resources does not suffice for promoting innovation and enterprise. These require another kind of resource, more social in nature. Haynes refers to this resource as social capital, which she conceptualises as trust between relevant economic agents. Networks of support and exchange form a necessary basis for this kind of enterprise.

Increased prosperity seems to have triggered a frenetic consumerism, particularly around Christmas time. This intensified, even extravagant, behaviour has been widely interpreted as an expression of the growing materialism of Ireland. Kieran Keohane and Carmen Kuhling offer a provocative re-interpretation of this phenomenon. They stress that higher levels of consumption have less to do with the market than with the phenomenon of gift giving, which is at the core of social integration. Once more, economic behaviour is deeply rooted in social relations, and the market plays a secondary role in this respect. The authors suggest that many aspects of social life in Ireland are organised according to such rules of reciprocal exchange.

The pull of the market has been difficult to resist for the Football Association of Ireland. Yielding to the logic of accumulation in the international sports arena, the FAI simply sold the television broadcasting rights for Irish international soccer matches to the highest bidder. This meant that such matches would no longer be broadcast live on national public television and people at home wishing to watch the match live would have to subscribe to Sky Sports. Mark O'Brien looks critically at the claim by the FAI that they are a private company entitled to maximise financial benefits. He points to the public nature of their undertaking, not only because they receive large public subsidies but also because of the nature of the service they provide. The selling of the television rights for Irish international matches constitutes an attempt to subject a public good embedded in the public domain to the logic of capital, and to relocate it in the marketplace of commercial broadcasting.

The tension between the demands made by the market on the one hand, and the aspiration for a socially inclusive society on the other hand, underlies Bryan Fanning's chapter. He expresses concern that Ireland is renewing and creating divisions in society based on differences of migrant status, ethnic group membership and right to citizenship. Many of Ireland's new immigrants are working in the unglamorous sectors of the Celtic Tiger economy, doing the jobs that the indigenous population are no longer willing to do. They are highly vulnerable to exploitation. Fanning counsels that in contemporary Irish society there is a growing disjuncture between citizenship and actual social membership, leading to new forms of social exclusion.

The displacement of representations

The second part of the book focuses on changes in the beliefs and values around which Irish society is organised and in accordance with which Irish people live their lives. In 2001, the relics of St Thérèse toured the dioceses of Ireland and attracted large crowds. This event took place at a particularly low moment in the history of the Catholic Church. It was initiated by a religious order and was hailed as marking a revival of the church. It sought to bring about such a revival through a reactivation of a more devotional form of religious worship, only tolerated by the institutional church. Richard O'Leary reviews this effort at reactivating religious feelings in the new Ireland outside of the bounds of both institutional religion and social conscience. But the success of the tour does not seem to have left a lasting legacy that might have contributed to a reconfiguring of religious practice in Ireland.

Farrel Corcoran examines the very ceremonial state funeral and re-interment of Kevin Barry and his compatriots in the Patriot Plot at Glasnevin Cemetery. He interprets this sombre replay as an attempt by the state to mobilise the memory of crucial events in the formation of independent Ireland. According to Corcoran, the very public enactment of the funeral speaks to the unresolved nature of Ireland's institutional memory of the origins of the state. This memory site is exploited, one may suspect, for various political purposes, but mainly to steady the current institutional order in Ireland. It is arguable whether this exercise in memory construction has managed to revive the issue of the Irish nation as an organising principle of contemporary Ireland.

Core beliefs, constitutive of social practices and institutions, are now challenged in a sustained way. None perhaps is more crucial than the set of beliefs about what it means to be a woman or a man in contemporary society. Dirk Schubotz and Bill Rolston observe the changes that are taking place among men in Northern Ireland. Drawing on a study of sexual attitudes and lifestyles among young men, they stress the reluctance of various institutions to move away from a male identity constructed around work and fatherhood, and their failure to embrace the multiplicity of masculinities.

Another core belief relates to the way societies deal with their natural environment. Stephen Quilley is interested in a popular natural amenity in Dublin. He highlights the conflict between the recreational use of the place and the protection of its wildlife. Pointing to the fact that Bull Island is the outcome of human intervention in Dublin Bay, the author argues that nature is not adequately perceived as a kind of objective and harmonious backdrop to human activity. It is shaped in the interaction between human societies and their environment. Humanity is also part of nature.

Going places

The reconfiguration of Ireland is not played solely around the tension between economic mechanisms and their social frame, or around the displacement of beliefs and representations. It is inscribed in the way space is socially organised and a sense of place structured. The capacity of enterprises to operate on the global market is deeply rooted in regional conditions, but also in the representation of the region. Ethel Crowley presents the case of Fuchsia Brands Ltd, which has been created as a brand name in West Cork in an attempt to sell quality regional products on the global market. The case study illustrates that globalisation does not necessarily or primarily operate through a standardisation of mass-produced goods. It can also take place through the production and marketing of distinctive regional products. But in order to succeed, the region must be represented and perceived in a way that upholds the qualities that are claimed by the brand.

Dublin, too, is elaborated as a very specific kind of place. Mary Corcoran points out how the reshaping of Dublin has in the recent past revolved to a large extent around the project of erecting a monument in O'Connell Street. The 'Spire of Dublin' is a key part of a regeneration policy for Dublin, boosting that part of the city lying to the north of the River Liffey. Furthermore, the Spire and the regeneration plan for O'Connell Street are part of a strategy to reconfigure the northside/southside division that has hitherto defined the image of the city. Public opinion has been sharply divided about the Spire. Some critics stress that it stands for nothing and is unconnected to the history or heritage of the city and the country. On the other hand, it is seen as having significant potential to become *the* symbolic icon for Dublin, a marker of both identity and place.

The successful making and marketing of some places implies that others remain non-places. Emre Işık considers the small midlands town of Rathdowney. Although not remote from Dublin in terms of distance, it has remained peripheral because it is located outside the high-speed world of consumerist Ireland. The recent opening of a designer discount outlet in Rathdowney can be seen as an attempt to increase the locality's speed and to relocate it within an ever-expanding circuit of consumption. Signposts and advertising billboards in the nearby large towns direct the passer-by to Rathdowney, literally putting it on the map. Rathdowney then is attempting to make the transition from a non-place to a some place.

One consequence of Dublin's outward development is the transformation of non-places into new forms of urban centre that have been referred to by some as edge cities. Michel Peillon argues that Dublin increasingly takes the form of a large conurbation, with a multiplicity of small centres performing a range of urban functions. It appears less and less useful to think of Dublin as a metropolis, with a downtown centre and sprawling suburbs. However, this does not necessarily mean that central Dublin is experiencing a decline. Simply, it functions less as a centre or point of orientation for those living in the wider conurbation.

Tensions and contraventions

The failure to draw on the cultural memory of Irish emigration in order to develop appropriate responses to present-day immigration is a theme explored by Gerard Boucher. He argues that new immigrants are frequently treated inconsistently and in a contradictory manner by social institutions, and that these contradictions extend also to their everyday social encounters with the Irish public. Rather than being welcomed, outsiders are kept at arm's length by the imposing conditions placed on the degree to which they can be included, integrated and accepted into

Irish society. The neo-liberal market approach to immigration, favoured by the Irish state, harks back to an earlier inward-looking economic nationalism. Furthermore, the widespread negative beliefs about immigrants militate against a more civil response to these new communities and their specific needs.

The vandalising of sculptures in the streets of Dublin constitutes a serious misuse of public space. James Wickham links this uncivil behaviour with the fact that inadequate public transport hinders access to the city centre. He relies on a comparative study of four cities, but particularly of Helsinki, to illustrate the car dependency in Dublin and the exclusion that it produces. He contends that such exclusion generates weak citizenship, low awareness of rights and duties within the public space and, consequently, a lack of civility within such a domain.

The incivility that is nowadays observed on the streets of Irish cities and towns sometimes takes the form of violent assault. Ciaran McCullagh contends that the reporting of such, sometimes fatal, acts of violence has turned into a moral panic. This seems to be triggered by the fact that many of these assaults are directed at young people, often students, with a middle-class background. Far from being random, such attacks may manifest a class tension felt particularly by those who have been left behind during the years of economic prosperity.

The street has been the scene for another kind of violent display. Most public protests and demonstrations in Ireland, organised by various groups and for diverse reasons, proceed in a peaceful manner. However, in May 2002, a Reclaim The Streets Street Party met with a violent response from the Garda Síochána. Joe Moffatt investigates the reasons why the gardaí reacted in such a violent way on this occasion. He considers a confluence of factors including the nature and style of the protest, the recent history of related protests in Dublin and the perception and orientations of the gardaí. These factors, he suggests, produced 'deviance amplification', prompting an out-of-the-ordinary response on the part of the gardaí.

The transformation of place is a key process in the reconfiguration of Ireland. A central theme running through this collection and linking the different contributions is the idea of place, and its opposite, non-place. This volume is concerned with the changing place of Ireland within a global order. It questions whether or not we still 'know our place' despite all the changes wrought in recent years. It also records some of the displacements in beliefs and practices which Ireland is experiencing. In recent years, our willingness to make a place for others in contemporary Irish society has been challenged. Ireland as a whole has become a non-place for some categories of people, that is a place from which they are barred and excluded.

The contributions focus on the making and re-making of places, be they in West Cork, Dublin or the midlands. Localities, regions and towns endeavour to enhance their profile and become a 'place'. The difference between place and non-place is often the possession of some crucial resource such as social capital, an aesthetically pleasing landscape or a particular place image. Sometimes, a 'nowhere' space becomes a place in its own right: a place that people know, recognise and travel to. In the reverse direction, spaces that were once publicly valued have become non-places. Witness what is happening in quintessential public places such as some of the streets in Irish towns and cities that have been given over to traffic, that no longer promote civility or that are deemed dangerous no-go areas. The public space of the street is now reclaimed in various ways in order to re-create it as a meaningful place.

The contributors to this volume invite you the reader to scrutinise the reconfiguration of Ireland as it unfolds in and around the twin co-ordinates of *Place and Non-Place*.

PART 1

MARKET SOCIETY?

Ogigia from focail.com by Seán Hillen and Ruán Magan, 2003

Tír gan Teanga from focail.com by Seán Hillen and Ruán Magan, 2003

Lookers by Cris Neumann, 2004, cardboard

Showhome by Nathan Coley, 2004

CHAPTER 2

Falling over the Competitive Edge

SEÁN Ó RIAIN

In the Celtic Tiger years of the 1990s, Ireland apparently rode the roller coaster of freewheeling capitalism towards the information society. A boom in high technology industry was said to be fuelled by a new entrepreneurial class competing in free markets, and driven forward by private investors motivated by low tax rates. Ireland was unusual too in that it turned to international investors as the source of economic change. Foreign investment in high technology was intensely promoted, stressing Ireland's attractions: a skilled English-speaking labour force, access to the EU market and, above all, low corporate tax rates. The untrammelled market remained the road to a coveted place in the brave new information economy.

This belief would have been all too familiar to Karl Polanyi, who wrote in the 1940s of the dangers of the 'liberal creed' that elevates markets above all other social relationships.[1] While markets can be important and useful institutions, creating a 'market society' that prioritises markets over relationships of community and social solidarity will ultimately lead to social fragmentation and even economic decline. Sustainable economic growth must remain embedded in social relationships – as markets

1 K. Polanyi, *The Great Transformation,* Boston: Beacon Press, 2001 [1944].

themselves tend to undermine the relationships of co-operation that are essential to social life and economic development. After World War II, many advanced capitalist countries, in Polanyian fashion, embedded market relationships firmly within national welfare state institutions and international controls on trade and capital flows. Since the 1970s, however, these social and political institutions have been under attack from a new, virulent form of the 'liberal creed', which advocates widespread deregulation, privatisation and reduced public spending.

A blind faith in the global market had come early to Ireland, with the turn to foreign investment and free trade in the 1950s. After the economic disasters of the 1980s, globalisation appeared kinder to Ireland in the 1990s with the Celtic Tiger boom. In 2002, however, the economy slowed, inflation rose, foreign investment rates declined and unemployment began to increase. Nonetheless, faith in the market society persisted. The widespread solution offered to these dilemmas was the restoration of cost competitiveness by reining in public spending and controlling wages. The barriers posed to market action by the public sector, social welfare and the demands of community and solidarity were to be stripped away.

On the road to the post-industrial economy

Both the diagnosis and the cure for the Irish economy stated above are mistaken. Clearly, a boom in foreign investment did drive the rapid expansion in growth and exports in the late 1990s. But many of the best-known foreign firms were simply moving goods through their Irish operations to take advantage of low tax rates, creating an entrepôt economy that provided an illusion of growth and development. Significant elements of the Celtic Tiger were a mirage.[2]

[2] P. Honohan, B. Maitre and C. Conroy, 'Invisible Entrepôt Activity in Irish Manufacturing', *Irish Banking Review*, Summer 1998, pp. 22-36.

Nonetheless, alongside this conjuring trick of the global economy, and often in the same firms, significant transformations occurred in the capabilities of the Irish economy. Spending on research and development increased, new forms of team production were adopted, the labour force became increasingly professionalised and productivity improved. Irish-owned firms grew and a number became important international companies: exporters and overseas investors in their own right.[3] Most significant were changes in the labour market: as employment rose dramatically, female labour participation increased, unemployment declined and mass emigration was reversed. As it turns out, these transformations were rooted in new sets of social institutions and alliances between groups within the state and society rather than in individual entrepreneurial action supported by freewheeling markets for money, labour and technology. If the Celtic Tiger was a mirage, it was also a surprisingly concrete set of changes in economic life and new social and organisational capacities for knowledge creation emerged.

Although the most high profile parts of the Irish economy are in high tech manufacturing, it is important to recognise that all manufacturing only accounted for approximately 18.6 per cent of total Irish employment in 2001 and for 14.5 per cent of the growth in employment between 1987 and 2001. The employment growth, which was the most impressive feature of the Irish economy in the decade to 2002, was only partly based, therefore, on transformations in manufacturing. It was also rooted in expanding social services employment and expanding local demand for business, retail, construction and personal services.

The Irish labour force has clearly undergone a structural shift since the 1970s, with a marked trend towards a 'post-industrial' workforce. In the 1990s, even as agricultural employment continued its steady decline, manufacturing

[3] S. Ó Riain, *The Politics of High Tech Growth*, Cambridge: Cambridge University Press, 2004.

grew at 3.6 per cent annually, while social services grew at 4.4 per cent and market services grew at 5.7 per cent.[4] The transformation looks more dramatic when we focus on key sectors such as insurance, finance and business services (incorporating financial services and software) and health and education: the only sectors to record steady employment growth in every decade since the 1970s. Taken together with the unprecedented employment creation of the 1990s, Ireland has undergone a rapid shift towards a post-Fordist economy and a post-industrial workforce – driven in large part by high tech manufacturing, producer services and social services.

Typically, this transformation is seen as being driven solely by foreign investment. But this ignores the growing sophistication of foreign firms in Ireland, and the ability of the local economy to absorb new forms of work and technology. Furthermore, a set of indigenous industries has emerged that is only partly driven by links to foreign investment in Ireland – most significantly, the software sector. In these industries, the role of local entrepreneurs was clearly important and this entrepreneurship was deeply embedded in the set of surrounding institutions that shaped and moulded it. Firms that received state grant aid did not seek the easy road of surviving on grants, but grew faster, exported earlier and were more likely to be involved in innovative activities and alliances. Private investment was remarkably unadventurous in supporting Irish high tech firms in the 1990s; the state was the risk-taking investor in these crucial early years, and private investment capital only flowed into indigenous high technology when the returns were relatively certain.

Furthermore, since the 1980s, a network of semi-public institutions had emerged (funded and sponsored by the Irish state and the EU and often linked to the universities) that supported innovation and research. Innovation centres,

---

[4] National Economic and Social Council (NESC), *An Investment in Quality: Services, Inclusion and Enterprise*, Dublin: NESC, 2002.

programmes in advanced technology, technology centres and other institutions were an important collective set of supports for individual technologists and business people. Indigenous firms emerged where these institutions existed to enable local actors to take advantage of the connections to foreign investment and foreign markets. Indeed, it seems highly likely that the foreign investment boom of the late 1990s was itself encouraged by the growing sophistication of the innovative capacities of the Irish economy.

If export competitiveness has driven Ireland part of the way down the road to the informational economy, it has gone hand-in-hand with public sector expansion of social services employment. Together, these twin drivers of economic development have generated huge local demand (since around 1994) resulting in rapid increases in employment in sectors such as personal services and construction. In any overall explanation of the dramatic expansion of employment in Ireland, we need to focus not only on foreign investment or even general export competitiveness, important though these have been, but on the interaction of those sectors with the rather more unfashionable public sector, where job expansion was instrumental in creating patterns of local demand that generated further employment increases. Ultimately, the significant transformations in the Celtic Tiger are not driven so much by freewheeling market capitalism, as by a set of politically constructed and institutionally supported state–society alliances, extending across institutions of innovation and social partnership. In many cases, these institutions have emerged despite the official ideology of the efficiency of market mechanisms and the moral superiority of individual entrepreneurship.

The competitiveness obsession and the threat to the Celtic Tiger

As growth and exports slowed dramatically in 2002 and unemployment began to rise, the airwaves were filled with calls to restore competitiveness in the Irish economy.

Indeed, competitiveness has been institutionalised as a national policy priority with the establishing of the National Competitiveness Council, which monitors almost any aspect of social and economic life for its implications for firm competitiveness. The focus of the competitiveness agenda has been the reduction of costs, and the policy mechanisms of choice to achieve this goal are wage restraint and reduced public spending.

Casting the problems of the Irish economy in terms of competitiveness inevitably leads to calls for a crackdown on excessive public spending and wages. But the Celtic Tiger years have made competing on costs an increasingly precarious proposition for Irish firms, as reflected in recent job losses in the traditional sectors of the economy. The agenda for the Irish economy must be one of upgrading, learning and innovation. The current economic difficulties in Ireland fundamentally reflect the dilemmas of managing a transition from a low wage to a high wage economy, and industrial upgrading has become not just a motor of development, however incomplete, but a necessity.

Wage competitiveness is, in any case, of uneven importance in the Irish economy. The most dynamic high tech sectors either rely more heavily on tax breaks than low wages or have seen rapidly rising wages, outside the scope of the national social partnership agreements. On the other hand, wages have remained all too low in many services sectors and it is perverse to call for further restraint. Where wage restraint has been most important is in the least sophisticated sectors of Irish industry and in managing the public sector pay bill to assist in reducing public debt. Calls for wage restraint do not address the complexities of the variety of upgrading strategies required in different sectors and the politics of balancing these sectoral differences within the national political economy.

Indeed, focusing on wage restraint directs policy attention away from investing in labour, learning and improved training, and long-term career development and security. A neo-liberal economic strategy, focused on a narrow concept of cost competitiveness, will seriously undermine this necessary upgrading: potentially generating a vicious circle of declining investment, rising inequality and ultimately the weakening of co-ordination capacities and the social basis of the knowledge economy. Nonetheless, this is the strategy that the Fianna Fáil and Progressive Democrats coalition government has pursued: cutting back on public spending (already at a remarkably low level compared to other countries) and in the process undermining the very institutions that had important developmental impacts in the Celtic Tiger years.

Similar problems arise in relation to cutbacks in public spending and low levels of long-term public investment; such policies are damaging Ireland's capacity to evolve as an information society. The education system is suffering as the decline in the numbers of young people in the population is seen as an opportunity for cost cutting in education rather than a chance to implement smaller class sizes and other forms of pedagogical best practice. Reduction in funding for research has threatened long-term organisational development in the universities, just as a new set of research institutions was being established. More broadly, students in primary and secondary schools have walked out of their classes to protest at the deteriorating physical condition of their school buildings. There is a perversity in a system that lauds the knowledge economy and society, while failing to support the very educational institutions – from primary to third level – that are crucial to building them.

Commercialisation and cutbacks have also undermined the network of innovation institutions that were important to the upgrading that took place in the 1990s. The Centre for Software Engineering (CSE) at Dublin City University has played an important and widely acknowledged role in promoting quality in software engineering. However, reduced public funding in recent years and cutbacks in funding to Dublin City University have left the CSE in deep financial trouble and facing closure or management buy-out. Despite wide university and industry recognition of the important role played by the CSE in developing the software industry, a critical part of the institutional infrastructure of this industry is being undermined by the priority put on cost containment over collective investment.

Ultimately, competitiveness measures have threatened industrial upgrading and innovation by weakening the social foundations of labour and learning. Costs have to be managed, but there is little evidence so far that market liberalisation has been successful in that area. Furthermore, just when sustained public investment in the long-term development of collective capabilities is more necessary than ever, it is undermined by reduced public spending and the blind implementation of market liberalisation.

The Celtic Tiger was a missed opportunity. The creation of innovative capacities in the Irish economy could have gone much further, but was limited by weak investment in social institutions of learning. Those institutions that did promote innovation in the Irish economy emerged in the gaps and spaces left by those institutions purely focused on attracting foreign investment. Rising inequality could have been tackled more decisively through a redistributive approach to tax and welfare and, more significantly, by building a more inclusive set of institutions to support learning and innovation. The economic growth of the 1990s offered the opportunity for creative social democratic politics, with the possibility of narrowing the gap between the working and middle classes while still rewarding the middle classes. However, the opposite occurred: while most groups in society saw significant improvements in their situation through the Celtic Tiger years, policies consistently favoured the middle classes over the working classes and contributed to increased inequality.

The institutions that were built in the 1990s to support innovation and promote social solidarity were always threatened by the official story of the Celtic Tiger as a market-driven economy – the Irish version of Polanyi's 'liberal creed'. During the boom years, these tensions were papered over by rapid growth and booming tax revenues. But, when tougher times hit, the choice between free markets, and innovation and equality was posed more starkly: will the information society in Ireland be unequal and based on low wage competition, or will a more egalitarian, deeper system of innovation be created? The contemporary obsession with competitiveness threatens the very institutions that made possible the most significant changes in the Celtic Tiger years. Nonetheless, the opportunities to tackle inequality and build a structure of indigenous innovation remain – if the process of building social and political institutions can be sustained in the face of the narrow competitiveness agenda.

Ireland and Finland on the road to the information society

Is it simply wishful thinking to believe that we can have an economy that combines export competitiveness with equality and that can sustain investment in a sophisticated innovation system and a developed, universalist welfare state? No, it is not. Finland provides an example of just such a state. Finland, which experienced a similar boom to Ireland in the late 1990s, has in many respects a more sophisticated information economy and is clearly more egalitarian than Ireland.

The generous and universalist Finnish welfare state helps maintain the skilled and healthy population that sustains the information economy, while the information economy helps pay for the welfare state. Sustained by significant and long-term public investment policies to support innovation and vibrant communities of technology developers, Finland has combined growth and equality, and is one of the most competitive economies in the world.[5] The Scandinavian economies also attract large amounts of foreign investment despite high tax rates and a strong welfare state – indeed

5 M. Castells and P. Himanen, *The Information Society and the Welfare State: The Finnish Model*, Oxford: Oxford University Press, 2003.

the investment they attract is much more sophisticated than that lured to Ireland by the promise of low taxes and transfer pricing alongside a skilled labour force.

Ultimately, the lessons of the Irish and Finnish cases are the same. Developing a successful information economy requires significant investment in the labour force as well as in the institutions that support learning and innovation. Informational capitalism rests firmly upon social institutions, even if those who benefit most from the informational economy fail to recognise the significance of those institutions. However, the chimera of the market remains stubbornly in place. Belief in the market is crucial to the new elites in defending their moral claim upon the rewards of the informational economy, but that ideology ultimately threatens the foundation of the economy itself.

The development of informational capitalism is not necessarily linked to rising social inequality. However, a better political and economic choice would be to create an egalitarian information society – by developing both strong social institutions of innovation to support business activities and strong welfare states and egalitarian economic structures to support the population. The competitiveness agenda of restricting public spending, restraining wages and liberalising markets will eventually undermine competitiveness. Whereas Ireland's competitiveness has fallen, Finland has made gains. Investing in education and welfare, directing resources towards the excluded and exploited, taking away the low wage/low skill options within the economy and democratising workplace institutions will not destroy competitiveness, but will enhance it – even as inequality is tackled.

Institutions developed in the Celtic Tiger years contain the seeds of an information society based on social innovation and egalitarianism. It is only when these institutions of innovation and social partnership are supported by sustained and universalist public investment that the promise of the information society can be realised. If Ireland is to build on the transformations of the Celtic

Tiger era, and not miss the opportunities it offers a second time around, it will have to break fundamentally with the neo-liberal policies and ideologies which have come to shape the Celtic Tiger's self-definition, but which ultimately threaten it.

CHAPTER 3

Social Capital and Regional Growth

AMANDA HAYNES

In November 2002, the Irish government published its first National Spatial Strategy, marking a watershed in Irish regional development policy. Ireland now has a framework for co-ordinating public planning and investment in order to achieve more balanced regional development. This advancement is in line with an increasing focus on regional development within the EU. In light of the development of an Irish spatial strategy, this chapter explores the significance of social capital for the mobilisation of regional resources. It examines, in particular, the concept of trust and illustrates its potential for realising sustainable regional growth through a case study of technology-based companies operating in Galway city. It will suggest that the significance of social capital as a policy instrument may be the crucial missing link in the National Spatial Strategy.

The National Spatial Strategy

The principal objective of the National Spatial Strategy (NSS) is to achieve balanced development in the regions. This is to be accomplished primarily through the development and linkage of strategic nodes, which have been identified as having 'sufficient scale and critical mass to attract significant investment and job opportunities'.[1] The five major regional urban centres (Dublin, Cork, Limerick/Shannon, Galway and Waterford) and four additional gateways (Letterkenny, Sligo, Dundalk and Athlone/Mullingar/Tullamore) form the core development nodes. These cities and towns were chosen because of their location, critical mass of labour, developed transportation, communications infrastructure and access to markets – factors that give them the potential to act as 'growth nodes' for trade and industry.[2] A further eleven urban centres were identified as hubs that will link the gateways to wider areas of the region.

The idea that the creation of critical mass will result in increased dynamism within the regions underpins the NSS. The advantages of agglomeration are viewed in the NSS as a function of the population and infrastructural density of a hub: 'The availability of a critical mass of labour and skills, underpinned by high quality business infrastructure is central to achieving competitiveness'.[3] Thus, the key mechanism for achieving sustainable development is identified as investment in the physical infrastructure both in and between the gateways and hubs (including transportation routes, communications linkages, housing and energy).

---

1 Department of the Environment and Local Government, 'Government Launches National Spatial Strategy', press release, 28 November 2002.

2 J. D. Fitz Gerald, I. Kearney, E. Morgenroth, *National Investment Priorities for the Period 2000-2006*, Dublin: Economic and Social Research Institute, 1999.

3 Department of the Environment and Local Government, *The National Spatial Strategy 2002-2020: People, Places and Potential*, Dublin: Department of Environment and Local Government, 2002, p. 35.

Is critical mass sufficient?

In the past, regional development policies have effectively focused on correcting the symptoms of disadvantage rather than addressing the underlying causes of disadvantage. The root of this approach lies in a focus on 'competitive growth'. According to this perspective, the national growth rate is viewed as a given, locational differences only act to determine how this growth will be distributed among regions. Regional policy based on this premise focuses not on the development of endogenous capacity at a regional level, but on the redistribution of activities and resources from stronger to weaker regions.

The NSS still retains elements of this 'competitive growth' policy. The core mechanism of the NSS regional policy is the redistribution of resources on the basis of a centralised framework for investment in order to improve the locational advantages of the regions, and attract inwards more investment, jobs and people. However, the NSS also aims to build up the critical mass of labour and skills, underpinned by high quality business infrastructure in urban centres, in order to generate self-sustaining regional economies. In essence, the NSS implies that drawing a critical mass/agglomeration of companies and people to an area will be sufficient to generate the 'advantages derived from exchange of information, collaboration, innovation, adoption of best practices and mobilisation of finance and skills'[4] that are key to sustainable regional economies. The argument presented in this chapter, however, suggests that the existence of an agglomeration alone may not be sufficient to ensure generative growth. Drawing on the insights of economic sociology, it is possible to demonstrate how social capital, when activated at regional level, stimulates the processes of exchange and collaboration that make for successful regional development.

4 ibid., p. 35.

Interactive learning

The NSS correctly identifies the significance of collaboration and information exchange for the sustainability of agglomerations. The viability and growth of higher value-added activities is intrinsically linked to competitiveness based on innovation. Furthermore, the growth of such activities is key to stable economic prosperity in increasingly costly business environments like Ireland. Even low value-added industries can only compete on the basis of low cost structures in the short term, eventually being replaced by lower cost regions. Innovation is now accepted as the key to competitive advantage, and firms increasingly see learning as one of their most significant activities.

Innovation, however, is the outcome not just of learning but of interactive learning. Innovation does not proceed in a strictly linear fashion. New knowledge may be generated at any stage of the production cycle, and by actors outside of the narrowly defined innovation process. Thus, the emergence of innovations is not attributable to any single actor or any single activity. It does not occur as the result of a single product development programme within an isolated firm. Rather, it is considered to be the outcome of interactive and reactive relations involving a variety of economic actors. For the firm, such relations may exist internationally, nationally or regionally. However, for the purpose of sustainable regional development there are clear advantages to exchanges at a regional level. The capacity for regional collaboration and co-operation is significant for embedding companies within their locality and for further developing critical mass. In a highly mobile, knowledge-oriented world, one of the main reasons behind a firm's choice of a specific location is its proximity to competitors and sources of innovation. Regions are also advantaged in interactive learning, because of the geographic co-location of companies. Co-location is a potential source of social capital, which in turn aids collaboration and exchange.

The significance of social capital

Economic sociology recognises that the economy neither exists nor operates in a vacuum. Rather, economic life is grounded in social life: economic actors are social actors and economic processes and decisions need to be examined in the context of broader social processes. This view gives weight to the idea that social relations are an important factor in the decision-making processes of economic actors. 'Social norms, institutions and networks of organisation' are key to the social content of economic action.[5] One of the most significant forms of social capital that actors may access through their social networks is trust.

Trust greatly enhances the efficiency of economic relations. In essence, trust greases the wheels of business. It facilitates exchange and co-operation under less restrictive conditions than would be required in the absence of trust. Mutual trust may reduce the necessity for legal contracts, for excessive monitoring, for hierarchical oversight and for the other forms of bureaucracy that can make economic relations, including learning, more cumbersome and less efficient.

Economic sociologists generally agree that a shared culture can facilitate the generation of trust. The existence of a shared set of norms, rules and conventions provides a common set of 'ground rules' for the conduct of economic relations. This shared culture enables the development of successful contacts with others, which in turn generates trust. Shared cultures are not necessarily national cultures; they may be generated as a consequence of shared membership of, for example, a corporation, an ethnic enclave, a religious grouping or a regional collectivity. The region may be viewed as a site in which a specific cultural milieu that facilitates trust relations is more likely to exist.

[5] M. Zafirovski, 'Economic Sociology in Retrospect and Prospect: In Search of its Identity with Economics and Sociology', *American Journal of Economics and Sociology*, vol. 58, no. 4, 1999, p.583-627, p. 593.

While common bases for understanding may exist above the level of region, shared cultures are in practice most likely to be developed through proximity and repeated interaction at the local or regional level. A shared culture, in this context, may include not just language, behaviour and custom, but conventions, norms and knowledge specific to the particular economic and social environment.

Given its smaller size relative to other kinds of agglomerations, the region encourages the generation of trust-based relations on the basis of the frequency and intensity of contact. Geographical distance, even within a one-kilometre radius, has been shown to affect the frequency of information flows between actors. The rate of contact falls as the distance apart increases.[6] The accessibility and dependability of geographically proximate ties enhance exchange. Moreover, even in the age of electronic media, face-to-face and telephone contact remain the most popular means of communication for research and technical co-operation.

In addition, defection is less likely within a regional site. For example, due to the smaller scale of the region and the likelihood of more dense networks of relations than at a national level, defection would become more widely known and the application of sanctions would be more likely to have a negative impact. Social capital 'reduces the risk of opportunistic behaviour by means of a common binding governance structure'.[7] This in turn facilitates the exchange of both codified and, more particularly, tacit knowledge.

Thus, the region possesses a number of advantages in terms of generating exchange and co-operation which are beneficial for the local business environment. These are the

6 D. Charles and J. Howells, *Technology Transfer in Europe: Public and Private Networks*, London: Belhaven Press, 1992, p. 47.

7 H-J. Braczyk and M. Heidenreich, 'Regional Governance Structures in a Globalised World', in H-J. Braczyk, P. Cooke and M. Hiedenreich (eds.), *Regional Innovation Systems*, London: UCL Press, 1998, pp. 414-440, p. 434.

factors cited by the NSS as central to the sustainability of regional agglomerations. However, it is not the mere presence of actors in proximity, but how successfully the agglomeration achieves 'systemic linkage and interactive communication among the innovation actors'[8] that determines the degree to which the system ultimately creates competitive advantage.

Harnessing social capital

Although social capital is a relatively new term, it has a long lineage within the sociological literature. More than a century ago, Durkheim observed that:

> A nation can be maintained only if, between the State and the individual, there is interconnected a whole series of secondary groups near enough to the individuals to attract them strongly in their sphere of action and drag them, in this way, into the general torrent of social life....[9]

At the level of the region, the intangible asset that is social capital is operationalised as associationalism, that is the degree to which 'the club, forum, working party, consortium or partnership model'[10] is in evidence. Whether voluntary, private or public, these associations are viewed as key to normalising interactive learning and to enabling the regionally based companies to take full advantage of the possibilities for strategic collective learning. More informal manifestations of social capital, such as unorganised knowledge networks, are also significant. While such

8 P. Cooke and K. Morgan, *The Associational Economy: Firms, Regions and Innovations*, New York: Oxford University Press, 1998, p. 71.

9 E. Durkin, *The Division of Labor in Society*, New York: The Free Press, 1964, p. 28.

10 P. Cooke, 'Introduction', in H-J. Braczyk, P. Cooke and M. Hiedenreich (eds.), *Regional Innovation Systems*, London: UCL Press, 1998, pp. 2-25, p. 10.

associations may arise spontaneously, they are more likely to take root when there is a culture of interactive learning already in existence. Specific strategies to assist the development of associational ties between actors are a key feature of successful regional development programmes. It is noteworthy, for example, that the Danish model cited as an exemplar by the NSS, includes in its industrial development strategy a transport forum, IT club, business magazine and exhibitions – all means of enhancing associational ties.

Social capital in the Galway ICT sector

A case study of information and communications technology (ICT) companies in Galway city reveals two important insights about regional development: the potential of social capital for mutually beneficial exchange and co-operation and the need for co-ordinating structures in order to harness its full potential.

The companies that participated in this case study maintained a myriad of personal contacts in the ICT cluster in Galway. Contacts had been developed and nurtured as a result of common employment in the same company or on the same contract, having worked for or having employed one another, or having been located in the same incubation centre or business park over a period of time. Extended or repeated interaction led to the development of familiarity, not only with a given individual's character but, more importantly, with their technical and professional capabilities. This familiarity enabled the assessment of the contact's abilities and reliability.

Where trusting relations had developed, the contact became valuable for sourcing information and skills. Mutual trust allowed case study participants to refer commercially sensitive questions, problems and work to their contacts. The trust-based relations on which the informal network was founded in this regional ICT sector was used for five main purposes: recruiting employees, acquiring contracts, assigning contracts, sourcing information and resources, and forming formal collaborative ventures.

Personal contacts were commonly used in recruitment, particularly where the post to be filled was of particular importance to the company. The informal network provided companies with access to information regarding the availability and suitability of staff. More importantly the network could provide information about those aspects of a potential employee's character and skills that might be difficult to glean from a curriculum vitae. Access to this informal stock of knowledge could, therefore, help to prevent costly hiring mistakes.

Personal contacts were, in a number of cases, a means for companies to source contracts. As with recruitment, the more locally embedded companies (in terms of founders' previous employment) were better able to access networks for this purpose. Companies that had moved into the locality generally had to resort to more traditional methods of seeking contracts. Highly specialised companies that lacked a potential customer-base in the region had to draw on other resources and wider networks to seek work. Nonetheless, local personal networks had been of assistance to a number of the more generically oriented companies in acquiring contracts, particularly in their start-up phases.

Significantly, however, the basis for the decision to award contracts to particular personal contacts was not loyalty or friendship, but the reassurance provided by one's knowledge of the contact's abilities – one's trust in them. Additional reasons for awarding contracts to known contacts included the desire to support local companies and the belief that personal relationships lead to the provision of a more responsive service. The award of contracts to personal contacts was not simply a form of 'nepotism'. Rather, it represented a strategy for reducing uncertainty by avoiding dealings with unknown or little-known companies.

The kinds of information and resources that companies accessed through the informal network were varied. In terms of resources, for example, some people in the Galway city ICT sector provided their skills for free to personal contacts, where the task undertaken was not perceived to be time consuming. Much more common, however, was information exchange. As with recruitment, the right information at the right time can prevent costly mistakes. In total, nine of the thirty companies surveyed specifically named other companies in the sample with whom they regularly exchanged information or mutual assistance based on informal rather than contractual linkages.

Furthermore, the informal network was activated to access experiential knowledge, information and references regarding issues peripheral to firms' core competencies. The informal network was cited as a source of knowledge regarding finance (including venture capital companies and state-funded equity capital), employment legislation, remuneration structures, and general organisation. The network served to provide referrals to useful private and public sector organisations. In terms of more specific technical knowledge, the informal network was frequently cited as a source of advice regarding business systems, including e-commerce, computer networks and telecommunications systems, the purchase of hardware and software and the choice of Internet service providers. The informal network functioned as a mechanism for reducing the uncertainty surrounding the multitude of decisions that companies must make. There was a feeling, particularly among those companies that had the most extensive and dense local networks and the most frequently used ties, that the network represented a support structure on which they could draw. This enabled them to make the best possible decision on peripheral technical and non-technical decisions. The reduction of uncertainty contributed to the broader context of innovation, because firms were in a position, through their informal knowledge networks, to enhance their human resources and externally sourced services and technology.

However, the regional environment did not generate a significant number of ties resulting in innovation in core competencies. For example, while half of the firms in the study were involved in some type of collaborative research and development/product development, only three had been involved in such formal relationships with other members of the Galway ICT sector. It was noteworthy that companies were amenable to forming such relationships locally where the appropriate competencies existed. A mismatch between the competencies and levels of expertise among local industry, spurred small and medium-sized enterprises (SMEs) to seek access to non-local research resources. However, it was also the case that all research and development/product development collaborations had been formed on the basis of vertical relationships, that is the firms involved had all been suppliers or customers of their partners. The potential for research relationships with horizontally related firms was underdeveloped.

Indeed, the majority of innovation linkages operate through the supply chain, which offers a pre-existing set of relationships that can more easily be developed into dynamic linkages for the purpose of innovation. Horizontal relationships, on the other hand, usually require activation. The presence of associations on the ground has been identified as a key catalyst in the emergence of horizontal innovation relationships, particularly between SMEs. In other regions, it has been necessary to purposefully activate the social capital in the locality in order to generate horizontal linkages. The presence of co-ordinating organisations within the region is key to this activation.

In 1999, when the fieldwork for this study was conducted, there were two relevant organisations geared to the development of the Galway ICT cluster. One of these was only beginning to actualise its potential, while the other was reported by study participants to be languishing, as a result of waning participation among its members, particularly the SMEs. Although participants were enthusiastic about deepening their links with local companies and indeed viewed collaboration as a necessity in a fast-moving sector, they simply did not have the time to invest. A significant impediment to the capacity of informal local networks to develop associative forms of organisation was the absence of local or national funding for such initiatives. The study participants felt that such funding would reduce the pressure on voluntary members to engage in organisation and administration.

Conclusion

The NSS notes that 'The establishment and strengthening of clusters will require the support of high quality education, skills and research, together with physical infrastructure'.[11] Certainly the NSS framework for investment in infrastructure will enhance the attractiveness of the regions to potential private sector investment. It may even indirectly aid the development of regional economic clusters by improving physical linkages between more dispersed networks. However, it does not establish concrete mechanisms to make full use of the potential of regional agglomeration: to transform critical mass of population and infrastructure (through, for example, the inter-relation, co-operation, association and exchange, which the NSS envisions) into sustainable regional growth; or to transform the agglomeration into a cluster, defined by systemic interlinkage.

Just as public investment in transportation and communication links can be a mechanism for public policy implementation with regard to regional development, so can public investment in social capital. Government can harness local social capital for its public policy purposes. While it may be the function of the state to supplement the assets of the region in order to enhance its attractiveness to selected agglomerations, regionally based bodies must have the

[11] Department of the Environment and Local Government, *The National Spatial Strategy 2002-2020: People, Places and Potential,* Dublin: Department of Environment and Local Government, 2002, p. 97.

capacity to support, in a tailored fashion, the relationships between the members of an agglomeration in order to promote communication and co-operation. Actors at the local level are more aware of the problems facing local industry and the solutions that are not only feasible but acceptable to local partners. They are more likely to be embedded in their localities than state-level actors and, as such, have a greater capacity to facilitate potential partners.

Regions with significant levels of associationalism generally have access to either compulsory public funding or regional government support. However, local government in Ireland does not possess the capacity to fund industrial associations, while the Chambers of Commerce of Ireland, like those in the UK and the US, are private law chambers and thus are confined to funding based on voluntary membership. In the past, national government has tended to restrict its funding to publicly run national networks. Support for regional associationalism would help to unlock the potential of social capital to spur economic growth in the regions.

CHAPTER 4

The "Gift" Relation and Irish Consumerism

KIERAN KEOHANE AND CARMEN KUHLING

According to a survey on consumer spending commissioned by Deloitte & Touche, Irish Christmas spending in 2001 outstripped that of all EU countries and even of the US. On average, the Irish spent €567 on gifts alone, compared to the European average of €446 and the US average of €561; and the Irish spent the largest amount on Christmas as a whole. This survey estimated that average Irish Christmas spending totalled €1,389 per household, including food and drinks (€280), clothes (€263) and socialising (€285) as well as gifts (*Business Plus*, 11 December 2002). In the words of Brendan Jennings, Head of Consumer Business at Deloitte & Touche, 'The proportion of Europeans celebrating Christmas is dropping, although not in Ireland ... Irish consumers appear to be planning to use Christmas to let off steam by spending significant amounts on gifts, food, drink, and socializing' (*Irish Examiner*, 11 December 2002).

Interestingly, this expenditure occurs despite the fact that the majority of Irish consumers surveyed admitted that the Irish economy was flat or in a recession (with 78 per cent holding this opinion) and felt that their own household economic situation would deteriorate or weaken over the next year. At Christmas, many lower-income families go into debt, a situation from which they may never recover. On 24 December 2002, the *Irish Examiner* reported that 'consumers face massive debts in spending spree hangover', and quoted Michael Culloty, spokesperson for the Money Advice and Budgeting Service (MABS), who reported that: 'some families on low incomes run up debts of around €2,500 and they are unable to pay ESB, gas, and phone bills in January'. MABS is a non-profit organisation that provides free advice to such individuals, and has been operating since 1992. According to Culloty, 'January and February are our busiest times ... people decide to splash out for Christmas and treat their children. They provide toys and designer clothes for their kids and they're faced with a huge debt at the beginning of the year'.

Also in 2002, the Director of Consumer Affairs, Carmel Foley, urged Irish consumers not to overspend at Christmas, and not to: 'overuse credit, since there is €1,300 million outstanding on Irish credit cards, which is double the amount 4 years ago and interest rates on cards is 7 per cent higher than the EU average' (*Irish Times*, 17 December 2002). Christmas spending has been steadily increasing since the late 1990s. 2001 spending figures were up 12 per cent on 2000 (*Irish Examiner*, 26 December 2001). Clearly, this cultural onus to spend at Christmas is at odds with the spending power of many individuals.

Crass consumerism?

For the most part, the response of commentators to what has been called 'panic spending' at Christmas (*Irish Examiner*, 18 December 2002) has been profoundly negative. The problem has been located either in some external influence on Irish culture, or in 'consumerism' – a practice that has been denounced as a symptom of the decline of Irish culture. For example, an *Irish Times* survey on Christmas 2002 asked: 'has Christmas been spoiled by crass commercialism?'. Many respondents exhibited an *externalisation* response, attributing mass consumer spending to factors such as the Americanisation of Ireland and the introduction of the euro. In a similar vein, a Unison.ie business poll on Budget 2002 asked the question: 'who is to blame for the high cost of living?', and found that while some blamed the euro, 9/11 and so on, others demonstrated a *denunciation* response, claiming that 'greed is endemic in Irish society' and 'we live in a greed culture'.[1] Whether reactions to Christmas spending adopted the externalisation or the denunciation approach, the majority of journalistic and public responses held that increased consumerism was a symptom of the decline of Irish values of community and family. They reflected a general belief that the eclipsing of such traditional values by consumerism was one of the risks of the recent growth experience in Ireland. A few respondents displayed a more self-reflexive (if cynical) taking of responsibility for this inflated pattern of consumption, as revealed in comments such as: 'Dunno, too busy shopping to give question any real consideration'; 'Yes, absolutely! Now excuse me while I finish the old shopping'; or 'Sure, but who cares?'. For the most part, responses reveal the nascent fear that Irish values of community and family are being eroded by crass consumerism.

Many recent texts have emphasised the negative effects of the Irish growth experience and have accurately documented how greater productivity has resulted in benefits for some, but has reinforced poverty and social exclusion for significant segments of the Irish population. This perspective is perhaps best represented by analyses from the Economic and Social Research Institute collected in *Bust to Boom? The Irish Experience of Growth and Inequality*.[2] Contributors to this book have outlined in detail the Irish growth experience and its social consequences. Broadly speaking, the analysts have assessed changes as

1 www.unison.ie/polls/index.php3?ident=Business&mypolii

2 B. Nolan, P. J. O'Connell, C. T. Whelan (eds.), *Bust to Boom? The Irish Experience of Growth and Inequality*, Dublin: Institute of Public Administration, 2000.

either positive (when greater productivity has led to increased labour force participation) or negative (when greater productivity has reinforced poverty and patterns of social exclusion).

The majority of sociological literature on the Celtic Tiger documents how the Irish growth experience has simultaneously produced both positive and negative economic effects, and thus has produced both continuity and change.[3] For instance, this period of growth has facilitated increased participation in the labour force for women, and has encouraged their entry into a number of occupations including managerial positions. But this growth has not reduced substantial wage gaps between men and women and the deeply entrenched patterns of segregated labour within the workforce or the home.[4] Similarly, other research has shown an overall increase in hourly wages in the period from 1987 to 1997, but also a widening of earnings dispersion, which means that this increase has favoured those at the top rather than those at the bottom.[5] More significantly, when inequality of distribution of disposable income in Ireland is examined in an international context, it is revealed that, despite rapid growth, Ireland has an exceptionally high level of inequality compared to other OECD countries, second only to the US.[6] The literature

3 D. O'Hearn, *Inside the Celtic Tiger: The Irish Economy and the Asian Model*, London: Pluto Press, 1998.

4 T. Fahey, H. Russell and E. Smyth, 'Gender Equality, Fertility Decline and Labour Market Patterns among Women in Ireland', in B. Nolan, P. J. O'Connell, C. T. Whelan (eds.), *Bust to Boom? The Irish Experience of Growth and Inequality*, Dublin: Institute of Public Administration, 2000.

5 A. Barrett, J. Fitz Gerald and B. Nolan, 'Earnings Inequality, Returns to Education and Low Pay', in B. Nolan, P. J. O'Connell, C. T. Whelan (eds.), *Bust to Boom? The Irish Experience of Growth and Inequality*, Dublin: Institute of Public Administration, 2000.

6 B. Nolan and B. Maitre, 'Income Inequality', in B. Nolan, P. J. O'Connell, C. T. Whelan (eds.), *Bust to Boom? The Irish Experience of Growth and Inequality*, Dublin: Institute of Public Administration, 2000.

demonstrates, quite rightly, how growth has resulted in both an increase in income levels as a whole and a rise in income inequality. It also highlights how increased rates of productivity in Ireland have not been accompanied by equitable forms of distribution; rather, it shows how the Irish growth experience has reinforced economic inequality, specifically as measured by individual and familial wages and income.

However, there has been a curious silence around the related issue of consumption. Inflated patterns of consumption are rarely examined in either the academic or popular realm. The evidence that does exist on consumer attitudes points towards the perspectives of externalisation (i.e. Americanisation) and denunciation (the intrusion of ‘greed culture’ into Irish society), both of which are seen as connoting a decline of Irish values. We wish to address this absence. We are interested in understanding what these changes in patterns of consumption reveal about the impact of the growth experience on national and individual character. The failure of academia and the media to address this issue reveals the paradox and ambivalence in Irish culture towards consumption. Given the strong public and journalistic outcry in Ireland about the intrusion of greed culture into Irish society, why is there such a contradiction between what people are actually spending, and the generalised condemnation of such over-inflated spending? Rather than simply condemning inflated patterns of consumption, we need an analysis that attempts to understand the motivations and mindset behind them.

Traditional generosity?

A clue to the answer perhaps lies in the response of a small group of people to the Christmas surveys. Some respondents argued that such spending was in our national interests since ‘encouraging Christmas spending will counteract the slowing down of the economy’. This latter comment expresses a fundamental aspect of the persistence of traditional communitarianism in modern Irish consumerism: shopping is understood as not simply selfish individualism, or even familialism, but as communal and moral, as contributing to the wellbeing of the collective social body. The diversity of responses illustrates that frenzied gift giving is a symptom of two contradictory moments in Irish society: on the one hand, the experience of increased spending power (at least for some) resulting from economic growth and, on the other hand, the persistence of the traditional system of gifting in Irish culture. This combination of acquisitive accumulation and generosity, of possessive individualism and collective commitment, coexists and collides in contemporary Ireland.

How might we interpret the extravagance of Irish gift giving, even on the cusp of economic recession? To do this we have drawn on Marcel Mauss's anthropological analysis of the 'potlatch' rituals of extravagant gift exchange amongst the Indians of the Pacific North West.[7] Mauss identifies a fundamental, general principle of economics as a total system of gift exchange, a system that is obligatory and reciprocal, and which functions primarily to institutionalise social solidarity. We will attempt to show the persistence of the 'gift relation' in the practices of consumerism in contemporary Ireland: what frequently appear to be the worst excesses of egoistic possessive individualism also show the persistence of a residual communitarianism, of a residual deep need for community and solidarity.

In traditional cultures, and in contexts of scarcity, extravagance is periodic and contained within the spatial, temporal and moral boundaries of reciprocal gift relations. Country people at a fair or on a holiday ought to be *flaithiúil* – extravagant; at weddings and funerals, food and drinks should be plentiful, in excess – *go flúirseach*. But this excess is to be understood in terms of wider cycles of scarcity, deprivation, obligatory reciprocation and continuity, in what Mauss identifies as a total system of gift exchange

7 M. Mauss, *The Gift*, London: Routledge, 2002 [1954].

pertaining to social systems such as the pre-modern Irish community. Thus, extravagant expenditure in the context of traditional community was a principled and morally sanctioned way of collectively disposing of what Bataille calls the 'accursed share',[8] the excess or 'surplus enjoyment' that is generated by, and sustains, all social life.

When the cyclical economy is replaced by linear progressive accumulation, the excess of cash persists vestigially as a problem of disposal. Peillon has shown how contemporary Irish festivals and celebrations, such as the Galway Arts Festival, the St Patrick's Festival and fireworks extravaganzas, are simulacra; new festivals manufactured by the tourism industry, which perform the function of blowing off and consuming the surplus generated by the boom.[9]

Shopping, as the central ritual activity of modern consumer culture, tends to displace and replace everything else, but its idiomatic content continues to display the unique and peculiar characteristics of local identity. In contemporary Ireland, instead of, or more typically as well as, going to Sunday mass, some families now go *en masse* to do the family shopping in the shopping centres, DIY superstores or home improvement centres that now open on Sundays. Extravagant expenditure on the home and on children is legitimated as morally justifiable within a traditional normative order: it is not selfish, but contributes actively to the material sustenance and reproduction of the traditional institutions of the home and family life.

Thus, the most fundamental function of shopping may be interpreted neither in terms simply of individual consumerism nor as a social activity with residual communitarian qualities, but in terms of the more

8 G. Bataille, *The Accursed Share: An Essay on General Economy*, New York: Zone, 1998.

9 M. Peillon, 'Carnival Ireland', in E. Slater and M. Peillon (eds.), *Memories of the Present: A Sociological Chronicle of Ireland, 1997–1998*, Dublin: Institute of Public Administration, 2000.

elementary and fundamental relations of the gift as described by Mauss. The rituals of family shopping, and its very excesses, function primarily to establish, maintain and reproduce obligatory and reciprocal relations of social solidarity. Shopping shores up and reinforces the collective representations of the traditional roles of the 'good provider', the 'good Irish mother' and the good of 'traditional Irish family life' to which we are all beholden and which have constituted elements of the collective consciousness in Ireland.

Against this background we can see the importance of the gift relation in reconciling the practices of Irish consumerism with more traditional aspects of our collective representations. The primary anxiety is that the new affluent Ireland is becoming less generous. Our collective representation has been that we are a generous people; that we give more than other (often far better-off) people; that we give more, per capita, to events such as Live Aid and other highly visible global charity drives; that we give more in terms of emigrants' labour to the building of the prosperity of Britain and America. By giving, we are therefore entitled to receive more in terms of subsidies from the EU and American investment. Foreign tourists come here to see how generous we are with our hospitality. In short, our honour, wealth and prestige are increased by the system of reciprocal and obligatory gift exchange in which we are involved. This is especially evident in 'the way in which we vie with one another in our presents of thanks, banquets, and weddings, and in simple invitations. We still feel the need to *revancherien*'.[10] Mauss's analysis is also relevant when critiquing the extravagance of Irish spending during the Christmas shopping period. That Christmas shopping is said to be 'out of control', however, again illustrates the extent to which spending is channelled into an activity and

[10] M. Mauss, *The Gift*, London: Routledge, 2002 [1954], pp. 8-9.

endorses Mauss's point: through reciprocal gift giving and exchange we support and ritualistically celebrate family and community.

Extravagance is also sanctioned where expenditure on weddings is concerned, since weddings involve the affirmation of family in the eyes of the community, two values presumed to be central to Irish identity. The extravagant wedding and its associated rituals – the engagement party; the wedding shower; the invitations; the stag and hen parties; the ceremony; the honour roles of best man, bridesmaids, maids of honour, pages, ushers and so on; the reception; the toasts; the 'afters'; the gifts – are all about the reciprocal and obligatory gift exchanges that consolidate solidarities of families, in-laws, friendships and communities. The participants are honoured by this mutual recognition; by the demonstration of shared collective representations of family, community and friendship; and by strong forms of sociability and solidarity. Weddings are competitive as well: people strive to outdo one another in extravagance, to give their guests 'the very best' on the expectation and assurance of obligatory reciprocity. The antagonistic competitive quality of this practice can go so far as the sumptuary destruction of accumulated wealth to outdo rivals, thereby constantly bidding up the price of social solidarity.

Far from indicating the devaluation of traditional values of community, Irish consumerism shows paradoxically how the traditional value of community remains central. In the context of social changes that are perceived to be threatening or inimical to traditional values, it can in fact lead to an increase in their premium, with extravagant expenditure shoring up values and social solidarities perceived as being endangered. Traditional and modern, and egoistic and communal elements in the contemporary extravagant Irish wedding collide in the gift relation. The obligatory and ritual practices of 'keeping up with the Joneses' are the contemporary continuation of the gift relation, an elementary way of establishing and consolidating social solidarity. But the inherent antagonism of the gift relation, its inflationary competitiveness, can become inimical to the very solidarity that it seeks to constitute.

The larger framework

In Mauss's analysis, the total system of gift exchange unifying pre-modern communities may be replaced eventually by a total system of obligatory exchange relations in modern society. The fully developed modern welfare state would be an example of such a system, where, in exchange for taxation and democratically legitimated power, the state apparatus distributes goods in the form of social security, education, health, welfare and so on. This is the fundamental principle underpinning the social contract of modern democracy, explicitly in the so-called 'new deal' of the mid-twentieth century, wherein the individual was incorporated in the collective social body 'from the cradle to the grave'.

In the case of modern Irish society, elements of the traditional system remain in place and compensate for the fact that the modern total system was never fully implemented. Mothers, families and communities, for example, care for their sick, disabled or elderly members, as services are chronically under-provided by the state. This role has also been filled by voluntary bodies, charities, and most especially (and now infamously) by religious institutions. At the present conjuncture, this arrangement is breaking down. The traditional total system is unravelling as a result of processes of individuation. This places increasing demands on the state to provide more adequate services, services which families, communities and the voluntary sector can no longer provide. And the modern total system, always underdeveloped and now suffering exponential demand, seeks to cut back expenditure on health and social welfare, to defer demand, and to limit claims to greater resources.

Conclusion

Contrary to popular belief, the extravagance of Irish spending for Christmas, weddings, housing and so forth reveals the persistence, rather than the erosion, of Irish values of community and family. However, the particular expression of these values is extremely problematic, since it ups the ante: driving up prices, making house ownership inaccessible to lower-income families, forcing deeper into debt those who cannot afford such extravagant spending at Christmas or for weddings. Irish people are, per capita, amongst the most deeply indebted in the Western world, borrowing heavily to fund their participation in consumerist gift exchange.

The 'potlatch' system of gifting is all too frequently viewed romantically, as expressing the laudable values of generosity, hospitality and the solidarity of community. From the perspective of anomic and individuated modern society, the ideal of community that the gift relation seems to uphold can appear attractive. But Mauss is at pains to emphasise the competitive and self-destructive tendencies in reciprocal extravagant expenditure; tendencies that the nostalgic gaze of modern society does not see. Even though it represents a continuation of the values of tradition, family and community, the gift relation reinforces social exclusion and increases the polarisation between rich and poor in Irish society. Furthermore, the persistence of the gift relation in Irish society paradoxically hides the need for a stronger and more equitable infrastructure of taxation and redistribution. The voluntary sector and the 'community' will be called upon again for their generous gifts to compensate for the failings of the social system.

CHAPTER 5

Selling Soccer

MARK O'BRIEN

In July 2002, the Football Association of Ireland (FAI) announced that it had sold the live television rights to the Republic of Ireland's home international fixtures during the period 2002 to 2006 to British Sky Broadcasting (BSkyB) for €7.5 million. In addition, the rights to delayed coverage of the internationals and coverage of the association's domestic league were sold to the independent commercial station TV3. The state's public service broadcaster, RTÉ, was left out in the cold, thereby ending a forty-year relationship. Only one-fifth of Irish homes had access to Sky Sports and, although the announcement was greeted with dismay in almost every quarter, the FAI described the deal as 'too good to turn down' (*The Irish Times*, 6 July 2002). If the deal had gone ahead, fans would have had to subscribe to Sky Sports to watch live coverage of their national team playing in the qualifiers for the 2004 European Championship and 2006 World Cup.

The business of sport

In 1996, Rupert Murdoch, Chairman of News Corporation and de facto owner of BSkyB, described sport as a 'battering ram' that could be used to break into new markets. According to Murdoch, sport overshadowed 'film and everything else in the entertainment genre'.[1] Indeed, compared to other content of mass appeal, sport is relatively inexpensive to produce and has plenty of drama and excitement. It is, usually, non-political, does not alienate viewers or advertisers and is hugely popular among advertisers' target audiences. Also, given its nature, sport is best viewed live, thus strengthening the *raison d'être* of the pay-per-view system.

The development of transnational communication technology has resulted in an increasingly reciprocal relationship between football associations and media organisations. Under pressure from both groups, UEFA (Union of European Football Associations) expanded the 1991-92 season of the European Champion's Cup to a league format, subsequently called the Champion's League. Over the next decade the competition was gradually expanded to include the second, third and fourth placed teams from certain national leagues – usually those with large television audiences. This has resulted in more fixtures featuring top European teams and therefore more pay-per-view matches and more advertising opportunities and revenue. Football has undoubtedly become another branch of the global entertainment industry – a visual commodity to be exploited for profit. In 1992, BSkyB paid the English Football Association £304 million in a five-year deal that secured the live television rights to the Premier Football League. This huge investment of media capital resulted in the league being restructured to yield a financial return. Games involving popular teams were moved to Monday nights and were broadcast only on Sky Sports. In 1997, another five-year deal worth £670 million resulted in high profile matches being moved to mid-week slots and being designated as pay-per-view fixtures.

But it has not all been plain sailing for Murdoch or the concept of pay-per-view. In 1998, BSkyB attempted to

1 E. Herman and R. McChesney, *The Global Media*, London: Cassell, 1997, p. 75.

purchase Manchester United Football Club, but shareholders and fans strongly opposed the plan. The Monopolies and Mergers Commission eventually blocked the purchase on the grounds that it would give the company an unfair advantage in securing television rights. Had the purchase gone ahead, BSkyB would have been in the monopolistic position of being both seller and buyer of such rights.

Audience opposition to pay-per-view or public indifference to sports that move to subscription channels is also not uncommon. In April 2002, Germany's largest media group, Kirch, declared bankruptcy. A significant factor in the collapse was the German public's refusal to subscribe for the right to watch the national football league. In 1996, the English Rugby Football Union agreed a five-year English internationals deal with BSkyB for £87.5 million. The move to a subscription channel saw ratings and public interest in the game decline so much that, in 2002, the BBC was granted delayed transmission rights in an attempt to reverse the decline.

Sport and national identity

Sport at international level is much more than just a business, it is also a ceremonial and highly visible expression of shared national identity that acts as a collective ritual for citizens. According to Benedict Anderson, nations are 'imagined communities' wherein citizens largely depend on common recognisable symbols that elicit a sense of affiliation with the state and with each other.[2] The spectacle of national symbols such as flags or anthems at international sporting fixtures creates such a sense of affiliation and loyalty in even the most fair-weather supporters. Mediated international sporting events thus provide a distinct cultural arena wherein national identity is imagined and thereby reinforced or challenged. Indeed,

2 B. Anderson, *Imagined Communities*, London: Verso, 1991.

the success of the Republic of Ireland's football team since the late 1980s has forced a rethink on the defining cultural characteristics of Irishness, given that for decades football was regarded as a foreign sport.

The complex process of globalisation – 'the intensification of world-wide social relations which link distinct localities in such a way that local happenings are shaped by events occurring miles and miles away and vice versa' – has impacted on the concept of national identity.[3] The development of a world satellite information system that transcends the constraints of time and space has fuelled this process. In the past, broadcasting organisations tended to be national in character, constrained within the boundaries of a nation and addressing a defined citizenry. Today, broadcast media have a more global character that cuts across national boundaries to produce new transnational networks of inclusion and exclusion – most visibly perhaps in the area of sport – and that may very well challenge the concepts of nation and national identity.

Such developments have given rise to the idea of post-national identity: through a process of exposure to alternative cultures and identities, individuals have a looser affiliation to the nation. Such an identity is typified not by rigidly defined characteristics, but by 'shifting cultural identities which correspond to the simultaneous integration of individuals into different and competing networks of relations'.[4] Identity nowadays is situated in multiple imagined communities, membership of which may be a function of taste, choice and commitment. These categories are fluid in relation to one another and indeterminate at the boundaries, so it is therefore possible for a person to be an avid fan of both Manchester United and the Irish football team without feeling any less Irish.

---

3 A. Giddens, *The Consequences of Modernity*, Cambridge: Polity Press, 1990, p. 64.

4 A. King, 'Football Fandom and Post-National Identity in the New Europe', *British Journal of Sociology*, vol. 51, no. 3, 2000, pp. 419-442, p. 420.

Rather than the nation becoming totally redundant, it is merely being continually re-imagined. The notional space that is the nation still becomes a meaningful setting that informs action when individuals in particular social networks invest that setting with significance – as happens when citizens support their national team. Thus the nation still occasionally becomes the symbol of the social network because it acts as a common cultural reservoir for members. That is why the sale of the television rights to the Republic's home internationals to a foreign subscription-based channel by the FAI raises fundamental questions about citizens' viewing rights of national events and the custody of cultural entities such as teams that represent the nation at international level.

Organisations such as the FAI sit precariously on the boundary where citizenship rights end and multinational commerce begins. The FAI's participation in international tournaments such as the World Cup is predicated on the fact that it represents the nation. Indeed, the concept of nationalism is one of the basic principles used by the FAI to attract sponsors and by broadcasters to attract viewers; and it is the symbols of the nation that give Irish internationals at Lansdowne Road their legitimacy. The Republic of Ireland team represents the nation, is composed of Irish nationals that wear a national strip, play in the presence of the President or Taoiseach, salute the national flag and sing the national anthem. The question is whether such occasions are the private property of the FAI or the common cultural property of the citizens of the state.

Added to this dependence on the symbols of state is the fact that for years previous to the FAI–BSkyB deal, citizens had made two indirect payments to watch their national team in action. First, the FAI is granted annual funding by the Irish Sports Council – paid for by the taxes that citizens pay to the state. And second, citizens also pay a licence fee to fund RTÉ the nation's public service broadcaster. So when RTÉ paid the FAI for broadcasting rights, it was again receiving money from the public. Although constituted as a private company, the FAI is thus inextricably dependent on the citizens of the state for its financial existence and on the nation itself for legitimacy at an international level.

A question of ownership

The FAI's assertion that the broadcasting rights for Irish international fixtures were the private property of the organisation to sell as it saw fit, raises the question of who really 'owns' national sporting events. There are various forms of ownership, the four most common being: pure common ownership, such as the symbols of nationhood that are shared among a citizenry; common ownership under government trusteeship, such as public libraries or public service broadcasting; private property under individual ownership; and private property under corporate ownership.[5] One of the most significant trends in modern society is the gradual shift from common ownership to private corporate ownership. This process is fuelled by the emergence of large profit-driven transnational media companies, for example News Corporation, whose huge resources have seen public service broadcasters such as RTÉ increasingly sidelined in the cut-throat competition for sports rights. In a similar vein, institutions that are amateur and in common ownership have come under market pressure to turn professional and reinvent themselves as corporate entities – the continuous speculation as to whether the Gaelic Athletic Association (GAA) will turn professional being a case in point.

As communications space is steadily privatised and media content and audiences are increasingly commodified, the common public interest is gradually subordinated to private commercial interest. In the case of the European Champion's Cup, the structure of the competition was

5 V. Mosco, *The Pay-Per Society*, Toronto: Garamond Press, 1989, p. 24.

changed to allow more fixtures between top teams. On the back of this, audiences were charged a pay-per-view fee before being packaged into demographic categories and sold on to advertisers, thus doubling the revenue stream for the media organisations concerned. Access to this increasingly privatised communications space thus becomes a privilege that consumers pay for, rather than a free entitlement predicated on citizenship. In other words, citizenship is defined not as a set of rights but in terms of purchasing power, a scenario that produces a two-tier information society: information rich and information poor.

As the FAI–BSkyB deal proved, private transnational companies have the scope and resources to acquire cultural events such as Irish international sporting fixtures. They shape their production and distribution so that both the game and the audience are turned into marketable commodities. The motive here, of course, is the extraction of a monetary profit rather than a contribution to the celebration and expression of national identity. Under the FAI–BSkyB deal, those who could not afford to subscribe to Sky Sports would have had to wait for the delayed coverage on TV3 (by which time the result would be known, thus diluting enjoyment of the game) or watch the game in a pub (an unsuitable venue for younger fans). But given that these international fixtures depend for their legitimacy on the symbols of nationhood that are still in common ownership, was the FAI treading on thin ice when it insisted that it 'owned' the Irish international fixtures?

Television without frontiers?

As public resistance to the FAI–BSkyB deal increased, the government announced its intention to compile a list of sporting events that by law would be broadcast on free-to-air terrestrial television, thus ensuring that they remained in common ownership. However, the government claimed that this list would not undo the FAI–BSkyB deal (*The Irish Times*, 9 July 2002).

The legal basis for the list was the 1997 EU Directive *Television Without Frontiers*. It allowed EU member states to ensure that television companies did 'not broadcast on an exclusive basis events which are regarded ... as being of major importance for society in such a way as to deprive a substantial proportion of the public ... of the possibility of following such events via live coverage or deferred coverage on free television'.[6] This provision sought to 'combine the preservation of general interests with the development of the market'.[7] Each member state had the option of drafting a list of designated events to be protected. Italy, Denmark, Britain, Germany and Austria had compiled such lists.

Similarly, the Irish government had passed the Broadcasting (Major Events Television Coverage) Act in 1999. The sole function of this legislation was to give a legal basis to the creation of a list of events that were of 'generally recognised distinct cultural importance' that would be made available to all citizens on free-to-air terrestrial television. Such a move would ensure that major sporting organisations, especially those in receipt of public funds, could not place their own financial gain ahead of the cultural rights of citizens to watch major sporting events. It would also have curtailed the process by which large transnational media companies paid extravagant prices for national or international events and then broadcast them on a pay-per-view basis. Although their consent was not required, the FAI, the Irish Rugby Football Union and the GAA all opposed the list on the grounds that it represented a restriction on their bargaining power in selling television rights. Despite this being the very objective of the legislation, no list had been compiled and the issue of protected events dropped off the political agenda until the FAI–BSkyB deal was announced.

6 European Commission, *Television Without Frontiers*, Luxembourg: Office for Official Publications of the European Communities, 1997, Article 3a.

7 ibid., p. 8.

It eventually fell, albeit indirectly, to the European Commission to restore the viewing rights of Irish citizens. When the Office of the Commissioner for Education and Culture was asked to comment on the FAI–BSkyB deal, it flatly contradicted the assertion that the government was powerless. According to the Commission, the government was free to draft a list without further consultation and it would apply retrospectively once approved by the Commission (*The Irish Times*, 11 July 2002). Faced with this very public intervention, the government was forced to act and announced its intention to publish a list of protected events that would apply retrospectively. The junior partner in government, the Progressive Democrats, hinted that should the FAI persist with the deal, it could lose its state funding. Sensing the turning tide, the GAA stated that it had no objection to the listing of its All-Ireland senior finals.

The FAI, however, persisted in its opposition and argued that 'market forces should determine which broadcaster should have the rights to televise sporting events' (*Sunday Business Post*, 25 August 2002). Despite the generous annual subvention it received from the public purse, the FAI proclaimed that the 'principle of a more liberal market' resulted in 'a better product for consumers' (*The Irish Times*, 13 July 2002). But the FAI seemed unaware that it was operating a monopoly in the marketplace by virtue of the fact that it was the sole organiser of soccer in the state. Would it have been so vocal in advocating a free market had another organisation initiated a tournament to compete with the FAI's domestic league or vied with the FAI for public funding? According to the FAI, sport is a business; and with generous government grants and lucrative television contracts up for grabs, the FAI holds a very dominant position in the marketplace. Perhaps some real competition would result in 'a better product for consumers'. The FAI also argued that the BSkyB deal would lead to more investment in grounds, extra youth initiatives and extra resources at senior coaching level – the exact reasons for which it is in receipt of public funds. In 2001, the FAI received €1.5 million from the public purse and was promised €62 million between 2002 and 2005 for its participation in the national stadium project.

Not for sale

The government eventually published its list of protected events two weeks after the FAI–BSkyB deal was announced. The list consisted of the Summer Olympic Games, the All-Ireland Senior Football and Hurling Finals, Ireland's games in the Six Nations Rugby Championship and in the Rugby World Cup, Ireland's home and away qualifying soccer games and final tournaments of the European Championship and World Cup, the Irish Derby and Grand National horse races, and the Nations Cup at the Dublin Horse Show. The list ensured that these sporting events would remain in common ownership and be available on free-to-air terrestrial television, be it RTÉ, TV3 or TG4. If the organisers of any of the above designated events had not agreed a contract with a qualifying broadcaster twenty-eight days before the event began, any qualifying broadcaster could apply for a High Court order directing that it be allowed to broadcast the event subject to an agreed payment. The list was forwarded to the European Commission, approved in January 2003 and enshrined in Irish law in March 2003.

While there may be a happy ending for Irish viewers in this instance, it merits little credit for the government. Despite having passed legislation to protect the viewing rights of citizens, it had backed down on its implementation when lobbied by the sporting bodies concerned. The government's claim that it was powerless to act after the announcement of the FAI–BSkyB deal was disingenuous. It begs the question of whose interests the government was most concerned with: those of the citizens that had elected it, those of powerful lobby groups such as the FAI and the GAA, or those of Rupert Murdoch whose newspaper titles have a wide circulation base in Ireland. The Irish public has the EU and not its own government to thank for restoring its viewing rights to national and international sporting events. Nevertheless, this episode marks a small victory for the cultural rights of Irish citizens living in an increasingly commercialised world.

CHAPTER 6

Denizens and Citizens

BRYAN FANNING

In 2002, the Irish government published a revised National Anti-Poverty Strategy in the form of a pamphlet entitled *Building an Inclusive Society*. It identified, for the first time, migrants and ethnic minorities as a specific target group for anti-poverty policy. It also set an overall objective of ensuring that such people are not more likely to experience poverty than majority group members. This category covers asylum seekers and immigrant 'guest' workers on non-transferable work permits. It includes people with lesser rights to state benefits, education and employment training than Irish or EU citizens. The goal of addressing poverty amongst migrants and ethnic minorities implies a new emphasis on the integration of immigrants not explicitly stated elsewhere in Irish government policy. In effect, it articulates a concern about future social stratification within Irish society on the basis of ethnicity.

An obvious tension exists between such a goal and the goals of existing immigration and asylum policies that often have explicit aims of ensuring that certain categories of migrants remain marginal. Immigration policies aimed at preventing migrants from becoming embedded in Irish society are at odds with the social inclusion and integration goals implicit in anti-poverty policies. These debates were not explicitly addressed in *Building an Inclusive Society*, but it noted: that ensuring that migrants and ethnic minorities do not experience disproportionate poverty necessitates 'fair and sensible immigration policies', that racism and related intolerance need to be tackled and that rights to equal treatment must be upheld. Beyond such general statements of principle the report set no specific targets. By contrast, distinct goals were set for other identified vulnerable target groups. The reason given for this disparity was that very little information was available about the socio-economic situation of foreign-born residents in Ireland. It was 'not possible therefore, to define specific targets for this group as a whole or for a particular ethnic group at this stage'.[1]

Immigrant inequality in Ireland

The composition of Irish society has changed considerably in recent years due to immigration. The 2002 Census identified 92 per cent (3,584,975) out of a total population of 3,858,495 as Irish nationals. This includes those who define themselves, using the sort of hyphenated labels employed in the US since the 1970s, as Irish-American or as Irish-English. They are most likely returned immigrants. More than 7 per cent of the population of the Republic of Ireland are not of Irish nationality. Of these, some 133,436 were nationals of other pre-enlargement EU countries, 23,105 were from non-EU European countries (including EU accession countries), 20,981 were from Africa, and 21,779 were from Asia. Ireland does not yet have as high a level of diversity as exists in Britain, where black and ethnic British people account for 12.5 per cent of the population. Unlike Britain, the black and ethnic population in Ireland is, to a considerable extent, part of a larger non-Irish, non-citizen

1 Government of Ireland, *Building an Inclusive Society: The Revised National Anti-Poverty Strategy*, Dublin: Government Publications, 2002, p. 16.

one. People from black and ethnic minority communities in Ireland are far less likely to have the rights and entitlements of citizens than they are in Britain, where many such communities from former colonies have been established for generations. Unable to acquire citizenship, migrants in Ireland are not yet in a position to become hyphenated Irish, should they wish to do so.

Despite the Census, relatively little is known about how different immigrant communities are faring in Ireland. It must be emphasised that migrants and ethnic minorities cannot be considered as one homogenous group. A number of different ethnic minority communities find themselves grouped under this banner. If the experiences of other countries tell us anything, it is that different immigrant communities often have very different experiences. An examination of ethnicity, racism and disadvantage in Britain from 1966 (when the first major survey was undertaken) to 1994 (when the fourth such survey was undertaken) reveals disparate experiences of poverty and disadvantage. A picture emerges of shifts in the fortunes of some ethnic groups over time and the ongoing marginalisation of others.[2] In other words, it is unhelpful to generalise about the impact of racism or discrimination on minority ethnic groups. At the same time it is crucial to acknowledge that ethnicity potentially affects people's life chances.

Research has shown that migrant and ethnic minority populations in the EU are disproportionately represented in forms of poor and insecure work and are disproportionately unemployed. Furthermore, these problems have continued with second and third generations of migrant-descended communities who have been born, raised and educated in EU member states. The experiences of other countries and mounting evidence in Ireland suggest that factors such as

[2] T. Modood, R. Berthood, J. Lakey, J. Nazroo, S. Patten, S. Virdee and S. Beishon, *Ethnic Minorities in Britain*, London: Policy Studies Institute, 1997.

racism and lesser access to rights and entitlements do negatively affect the life chances of immigrants. They suggest that there will be inequalities within ethnic groups on the basis of class and gender and that some groups will encounter barriers not necessarily encountered by others.

Immigrant workers, immigrants with Irish-born children, people with refugee status and asylum seekers are each deemed by the state to have different levels of rights and entitlements. In all cases, these are less than the entitlements of citizens. Distinctions between the entitlements of a number of such non-citizen groups are the result of state decisions that categorise and stratify people for administrative and political purposes. A number of studies undertaken in Ireland in recent years have demonstrated how lesser rights and entitlements affect migrants according to the administrative category they find themselves in. In a 1999 study of asylum seekers, 95 per cent of respondents identified racial discrimination as a problem. However, the study also found that enforced unemployment due to the lack of a right to work seriously affected psychological, social and general wellbeing.[3] Another study undertaken around the same time found that the Bosnian community, composed for the most part of programme refugees with the right to work, had an unemployment rate of 40 per cent.[4] This was about ten times the national rate. The study suggested that a lack of access to affordable social housing by Bosnians contributed to welfare dependency. Many were caught in a poverty trap in Dublin's private rented sector and were unable to get by without rent allowances. As put by one respondent: 'Accommodation is the main reason why people can't work, the rents are too expensive'. Another likened insecurity of tenure to the experience of having been displaced as a

3 M. G. Begley, C. Gavaran, M. Condon, I. Kelly, K. Holland and A. Staines, *Asylum in Ireland: A Public Health Perspective*, Dublin: University College Dublin, 1999.

4 S. Bradley, *From Bosnia to Ireland's Private Sector*, Dublin: Clann Housing Association, 1999.

refugee: 'I have a feeling of being homeless in Bosnia and in Ireland'.

Concerns about discrimination

A number of submissions to the revised national anti-poverty strategy consultation process from bodies such as the National Consultative Committee on Racism and Interculturalism, the Irish Refugee Council and the National Women's Council of Ireland have argued that racism, discrimination and lesser rights may be causes of labour market disadvantage, joblessness, poor health, housing deprivation and social exclusion. For example, the submission of the National Women's Council of Ireland highlighted how discrimination could result from the intersection of lesser rights with gender and ethnic inequalities:

> The continuing Government prohibition preventing asylum-seekers from accessing employment reinforces the risk of poverty for a group of women experiencing economic vulnerability. Certain anecdotal evidence already suggests that these women are at risk of exploitation by employers recruiting workers in the black economy. It can be expected that women asylum-seekers and their families will remain in situations of severe disadvantage if the Government does not ease its ban prohibiting them from accessing employment.[5]

An Irish Business and Employers Confederation (IBEC) study of barriers to employment encountered by persons with refugee status found that racism was identified by respondents as the main barrier to obtaining employment in Ireland (see Table 1). Yet racism emerged as but one of a number of potential barriers.

[5] National Women's Council of Ireland, 'Submission to the Review of the National Anti-Poverty Strategy', March 2001, p. 17.

Table 1. Top 10 barriers to employment identified by refugees

Rank	*Barriers to obtaining employment*
1	Racism
2	Lack of skills
3	Lack of information
4	Cultural difficulties
5	Verification of qualifications
6	Transferability of qualifications
7	Lack of childcare facilities
8	Loss of health board housing subsidy
9	Lack of English
10	Other

Source: IBEC Survey Unit, *Employment of Non-EU Nationals / Refugees in Ireland*, Dublin: Interact Ireland, 2000, p. 21. Adapted from the submission by the NCCRI to the revised national anti-poverty strategy consultation process, which cited this research.

Another 2000 study of a cohort of more than 3,000 asylum seekers granted the right to work (the only such group to date) found that experiences of discrimination in employment were exacerbated by lesser entitlements to state-funded employment training and support.[6] Respondents in this case were not entitled to the types of support necessary to address the kinds of barriers identified by respondents in the IBEC study.

In 2001, concerns about the widespread exploitation of 'third country' workers emerged in the Irish media. For example, there were reports of Filipino nurses being paid 30 per cent less than their Irish equivalents and forced to live five or six to a room. Claims were made that some nurses who objected to working eighteen-hour shifts without any meal breaks were threatened with deportation. In March 2001, Labour Affairs Minister Tom Kitt issued a statement

6 B. Fanning, S. Loyal and C. Staunton, *Asylum Seekers and the Right to Work in Ireland*, Dublin: Irish Refugee Council, 2000.

that employment rights legislation applied to all 1.8 million people working in Ireland whether they were Irish citizens or otherwise (*Irish Examiner*, 4 June 2001). Various trades unions, including the Building and Allied Trades Union (BATU), expressed concern about inadequate enforcement of legislation. However, they also argued that the work permit system rendered immigrant workers vulnerable to exploitation.

On 8 May 2002, a Dáil debate on migrant workers referred to 'systematic exploitation over a wide range of sectors' and noted that the problem was particularly acute in the hotel and catering sectors, the meat industry and agri-related outdoor activities. It noted, again, that numerous cases of exploitation of foreign nursing staff had been highlighted. Complaints from immigrant workers included long hours, no overtime pay, having to work Sundays and at weekends for no extra pay, and general insecurity with respect to conditions of employment. As explained by Deputy Charles Flanagan:

> Many people are fearful of making a complaint lest they suffer deportation from the State. I know employees who have been told that if they bring a complaint to the authorities, they will be sent home immediately and will not have the opportunity to work any longer in the State (*Dáil Debates*, 8 May 2001).

Minority ethnic groups consisting of immigrants from outside the European Economic Area seem to be particularly vulnerable to racism in employment and at risk of income poverty as a result of discrimination in employment.

The gold standard of citizenship

Social policy aspirations for the inclusion of vulnerable or unequally treated groups in society tend to be framed in relation to the gold standard of full and equal citizenship. As put by T. H Marshall in 1950:

> Citizenship is a status bestowed on those who are full members of the community. All those who possess the status are equal with respect to the rights and duties with which the status is endowed. There is no universal principle which determines what those rights and duties should be, but societies in which citizenship is a developing institution create an image of ideal citizenship against which achievement can be measured and towards which aspiration can be directed.[7]

Marshall defined social citizenship as the right to share to the full in the social heritage and to live the life of a civilised being according to the standards prevailing in the society. The very idea of social citizenship is challenged by immigration. Joppke argues that in societies with well-developed social rights, citizenship becomes a precondition of inclusion. Those without such rights become relatively deprived of key resources needed to ensure social reproduction. The story of the last few centuries has been the gradual inclusion of more and more members of society within citizenship – for instance through extending the franchise and affirming the rights of women. In twenty-first century Ireland, there is a growing disjuncture between citizenship and actual social membership. Gradations of rights between citizens and non-citizens, immigrant 'guest' workers, 'illegal' workers, refugees and asylum seekers have emerged in a number of Western countries that, as recently as a century ago, operated few restrictions on immigration. In such a context, citizenship becomes 'not just a set of rights, but also a mechanism of exclusion'.[8]

---

7 T. H. Marshall, 'Citizenship and Social Class', in T. H. Marshall and T. Bottomore (eds.), *Citizenship and Social Class*, London: Pluto Press, 1996, p. 110.

8 C. Joppke, 'How Immigration is Changing Citizenship: A Comparative View', *Ethnic and Racial Studies*, vol. 22, no. 4, 1999, pp. 629-632, p. 629.

The presence of undocumented or illegal immigrants is inevitable when, in an era of high population movement, Western countries have restrictive immigration policies. Yet the majority of illegal immigrants in Western countries are from the same nationality groups as the legal population of immigrants, be they Mexicans or Irish in the US or Turks in Germany. Legal and illegal immigrants migrate to similar places for similar purposes. Illegal immigrants are typically minorities within regularised immigrant communities.[9] They are likely to be vulnerable and marginal members of such communities. In some cases they may be dependants of legal immigrants who have not been permitted to accompany them. For example, immigrant workers not permitted to bring their children into Ireland may do so anyway. Such interrelationships between legal and undocumented immigrants have implications for anti-poverty and social inclusion policies in terms of high dependency ratios and low household incomes. Members of minority ethnic groups without economic rights may have to work illegally or engage in marginal forms of entrepreneurial activity. Undocumented immigrants are particularly vulnerable to poverty and social exclusion.

Research published by the European Commission has emphasised that the lives of migrants are often fraught with risks not encountered by established groups. For example, immigrants seeking to establish businesses are compelled to incur higher levels of risk with lesser resources and fewer supports than indigenous entrepreneurs.[10] There is some evidence that minority ethnic groups encounter such risks in Ireland. During 2000 most of the shops run by immigrants in the north inner-city area of Dublin were

[9] S. Sassen, *Guests and Aliens*, New York: The New Press, 1999, p. 143.

[10] H. Cremer-Schäfer, C. Pelikan, A. Pilgram, H. Steinert, I. Taylor and G. Vobruba, *Social Exclusion as a Multidimensional Process: Subcultural and Formally Assisted Strategies of Coping With and Avoiding Social Exclusion*, Brussels: European Commission, Targeted Socio-Economic Research (TSER) SOE1-CT98-2048), 2001, p. 3.

vandalised in racist attacks on at least one occasion (*Metro Éireann*, May 2000; *Statewatch*, 10 February 2000). Racism can be a barrier to self-employment as well as to other forms of employment.

Integration, social inclusion and social citizenship

The National Anti-Poverty Strategy, since its inception in 1997, has emphasised the concept of social exclusion. In effect, social exclusion is seen as a consequence of the relative material deprivation that can result from income poverty and unemployment. At the heart of Irish anti-poverty policy is the thesis that due to inadequate income and resources some people may be excluded from activities that are considered the norm for other people in society. Many of the problems faced by socially excluded individuals, families and communities relate to social reproduction. For instance, marginalised communities face greater risks of being failed by the education system than those with above-average means and supports. An explicit relationship between social stratification and welfare stratification is evident within Ireland's formally two-tiered health system.

Increasingly, debates about social inclusion have converged with debates about integration. This latter concept is usually defined as a form of multiculturalism. It suggests that minority groups should be able to participate fully in society without having to surrender cultural distinctiveness. It also implies the need to remove institutional barriers that create structural inequalities inhibiting full participation. The debate about multiculturalism has generally focused on the need for further measures *in addition to* full citizenship rights. In this context, a number of recent European-wide studies of social exclusion and social diversity view rights as a prerequisite for social inclusion. As explained in one such study:

> We understand the problems of social exclusion and the possibilities for social inclusion in terms of the problems

> and possibilities of access to social rights. For our purposes the key social rights and packages of social goods are those relating to work, income and recognition. We refer to these rights and social goods as 'personal social capital' ... and as 'forms' of inclusion.[11]

Social rights as such are deemed vital to the promotion of the social inclusion of migrants and ethnic minorities. Indeed, a family resemblance is to be found between the goals implicit in the concepts of integration, social inclusion and full social citizenship. Each is at odds with the stratification of rights and entitlements and in opposition to the reproduction of social inequalities by public policies.

Discrimination becomes all too possible where immigrant workers have lesser rights and entitlements than citizen workers. Some forms of discrimination might be understood as a consequence of racism. However, racism represents one potential cause, amongst others, of poverty and social exclusion. In practice, racist discrimination covers a range of social, economic and political processes. When those affected by racism have lesser rights and entitlements than the majority group members, the aspirations of *Building an Inclusive Society* become a tall order indeed.

[11] M. Roche, *Comparative Social Inclusion Policies and Citizenship in Europe: Towards a New European Social Model*, Brussels: European Commission, Targeted Socio-Economic Research (TSER) SOE2-CT97-3059, 2000, p. 17.

PART 2

DISPLACED REPRESENTATIONS

Emotional Response Unit Icons by Steve Powers, 2003

Delux Dinghao by Clive Murphy, 2001, public intervention

Details from *NOW:HERE* by Garrett Phelan, 2003, permanent marker on wall, Dublin City Council flat

Details from *NOW:HERE* by Garrett Phelan, 2003, permanent marker on wall, Dublin City Council flat

CHAPTER 7

The Relics of St Thérèse

RICHARD O'LEARY

The Roman Catholic Church in Ireland has endured a very difficult period in recent years. As each new sexual scandal involving religious personnel became known to the public, many commentators described the church as being in crisis. The situation was exacerbated by a background of declining attendance at Mass, a collapse in religious vocations, and further distancing between the state and the institutional church. Together, these could be interpreted as signs of the belated arrival of secularisation in Ireland. 2001 started no differently, with the continuation of negative news headlines about the church. Then in April, quite unexpectedly, a different news story about Catholicism made the headlines. The relics of St Thérèse of Lisieux began a nationwide tour of the country. What took place over the following eleven weeks was a major religious and national event. Huge crowds all over Ireland came to view the relics in a public display of religion not witnessed since the papal visit twenty-two years earlier. The excitement was captured by headlines such as 'Thérèse frenzy hits Cork' (*Evening Echo*, 20 June 2001). Here, at last, was a good news story for a demoralised Catholic faithful and an institutional church under siege. But what does this event tell us about religion in contemporary Ireland?

Given the large attendance and the widespread publicity, many readers will be aware of St Thérèse and the tour of her relics, so a very brief summary will suffice here. St Thérèse was born and lived in France in the latter half of the nineteenth century. She joined the Carmelite order of nuns in Lisieux, was known to live a holy life and wrote reflections on religious life before her early death in 1897. Her autobiography has been an international best seller and she was canonised in 1925. St Thérèse is a widely revered Catholic saint and her bodily remains at Lisieux have become a major site of pilgrimage. The reliquary containing some of her bones arrived in Rosslare on Easter Sunday 15 April 2001 and was on a countrywide tour until 2 July. It visited eighty official venues including centres of the Carmelite order and all the diocesan Catholic cathedrals. At each location, the casket containing the relics was put on public display. The numbers of people turning out to visit the reliquary all over the country were clearly very large. Church estimates claim that three million people or as many as three-quarters of the Catholic population on the island joined the tour. While we cannot accurately quantify the numbers, or confirm this possibly rather high estimate, it was without question an exceptionally well attended event.

A religious revival?

An early assessment was made by the tour's national co-ordinator, Fr Linus Ryan. Fr Ryan is reported as saying that, prior to the tour, he had been 'concerned that after years of rapid economic growth, Ireland might be losing touch with religion' but, in light of the visit, 'We have to conclude that material things are not giving people what they hoped for ... There is a great spiritual hunger out there'.[1] A Catholic bishop, Bishop Hegarty, is reported as

1 http://news.bbc.co.uk/1/hi/northern_ireland/1358397.stm

saying that: 'It marks the beginning of a new epoch'.[2] On 1 May 2001, the *Irish Independent* published a headline asking the question: 'Is the Church making a comeback?'. The tour's success certainly raises some questions about contemporary Ireland, for example: does it contradict the claim that Ireland has been experiencing religious decline and is becoming a more secular society?

Many sociologists trying to make sense of religious change in modernising societies have found the secularisation thesis to be an insightful explanatory tool.[3] Within the thesis is the view that as societies become more urban and less agricultural, and their people more geographically mobile and better educated, there will be a decline in religious practices such as church attendance and in orthodox religious beliefs. Religious practice is viewed as being precarious in the more anonymous urban environments compared to smaller-scale agriculturally based communities. Geographical mobility and participation in higher education may disrupt institutionally based religious practice and bring people into contact with alternative religious and secular ideas that may weaken their beliefs. Secular thinking weakens religious traditions and prioritises scientific rationality. The processes of urbanisation, industrialisation, geographical mobility and expansion of higher education have been highly instrumental in fomenting the very changes that have been taking place in Ireland in recent decades, and especially in the era of the Celtic Tiger. Sociologists in Ireland have already identified a rise in the proportion of the population declaring no religious affiliation, a sharp decline in attendance at Mass, and a smaller decline in orthodox Christian beliefs. It is in this context and set against this thesis that the tour of the relics of St Thérèse can be examined.

2 D. Mullan, *A Gift of Roses*, Dublin: Wolfhound Press, 2001, p. 17.

3 See, for example, B. Wilson, *Religion in Sociological Perspective*, Oxford: Oxford University Press, 1982.

We do not have to resort to an entirely indigenous explanation of the success of the tour of the relics. The relics also attracted large crowds on recent visits to the US and to Australia. Therefore, the phenomenon is not unique to Ireland. Ireland is, of course, different from these other countries in that a large majority of the population of the island is Catholic, a majority of which attend church on a regular basis. Furthermore, the tour organiser noted how the organisational arrangements for the Irish tour had been effective in achieving such an impressive turnout in comparison to tours in other countries. The tour was lengthy (eleven weeks) and accessible (visiting more than eighty venues around the country). In addition, many venues had extended access hours, including all-night vigils. Even the form of the event was accessible to persons who might not be regular churchgoers; according to Fr Ryan, liturgies were reduced to a minimum in order to focus on the veneration of the relics. The organisational achievement in itself is instructive as it illustrates the enduring organisational capacities of Irish Catholics, especially lay people at local level, despite the decline in attendance at Mass and the demoralising criticism of the institutional church. However, an even more important consideration is the persistence of non-institutional or popular religious devotion in Ireland.

The persistence of popular devotion to saints

There is an ancient tradition in Ireland of popular devotion to saints. I do not simply mean the tradition of devotional prayer held in churches and promoted by the institutional Catholic Church since the latter half of the nineteenth century. Rather I refer to the older tradition associated with pilgrimage, relics and healing. St Thérèse and the tour of her relics can be seen to fit within this tradition. This tradition is believed to have drawn on pre-Catholic forms of religious practice and, indeed, was to a considerable degree submerged by the drive of the institutional Catholic Church towards religious orthodoxy in belief and institutional control over practice, especially in the post-Famine period. That modernising drive never eradicated the older tradition and now, as the institutional hold of the Irish Catholic Church is weakening, the persistence of less institutional forms of religion may again be more apparent. This is instructive as it reminds us that the decline of institutional religion, with its emphasis on formal ritual and hierarchical organisational control, may be substituted not only by individuals adopting new unorthodox practices in worship[4] but also by a reversion to older pre-institutional devotional practices.

St Thérèse is a saint to whom Catholics can relate independently of the institutional Catholic Church. Many Irish persons have statues of the saint in their homes, and so it has not even been necessary to go to church to petition her. Indeed, the tour was not formally organised by the Irish Catholic hierarchy. The initiative for the tour came from a Carmelite priest, Fr Ryan, and not the Irish Catholic bishops, although out of propriety the formal invitation to visit Ireland was issued by the Irish Bishop's Conference. Only one bishop was prominent during the tour and that was in his capacity as a member of the organising committee.

Greeley and Ward have noted that – in spite of falling attendance at Mass, low confidence in the church and disaffection from Catholic teaching – relatively high levels of devotion to Mary, the mother of Jesus, have persisted in Ireland.[5] The persistence of devotion to a saint like Thérèse is consistent with this. Furthermore, St Thérèse, while always a popular saint in Ireland, might have particular appeal in the current social climate. St Thérèse has an

4 See, for instance, the chapter on Intercommunion by the author in volume two of this series: R. O'Leary, 'The President's Communion', in E. Slater and M. Peillon (eds.), *Memories of the Present: A Sociological Chronicle of Ireland, 1997–1998*, Dublin: Institute of Public Administration, 2000.

5 A. Greeley and C. Ward, 'How Secular is the Ireland we live in?', *Doctrine and Life*, vol. 50, no. 10, 2000.

impeccable reputation as a virtuous person, a reputation that has not been besmirched by the scandals that have damaged the institutional church. Indeed, it is possible that the wider context of scandal surrounding the institutional church and corruption in political and other spheres of life makes the uncorrupted personage of St Thérèse seem all the more attractive and worthy of veneration. This may be amplified by her association with the Carmelites, a religious order with a favourable and scandal-free reputation in Ireland.

If it is the case that not all traditions are abandoned in modern society, we can proceed to question why people choose to maintain some rather than other traditions. Why is the tradition of petitioning St Thérèse so enduring? What do people want from St Thérèse? As with any large-scale gathering of the public, it is reasonable to expect that there was a broad range of motivations among those present. For many it was clearly a deeply personal spiritual occasion, the meaning of which cannot easily be explored here. However, some of those who attended St Thérèse devotions have expressed the reasons for their attendance and these can provide us with some insights.

When asked about any abiding memories of the tour, Fr Ryan specifically mentioned the number of sick persons present, which emphasises the appeal to persons suffering from ill health. Among the letters sent to Don Mullan for his commemorative book on the visit were accounts such as:

> A child wrote: 'I used my white cloth to touch the casket. [Later] I was very sick with a touch of malaria. My mother rubbed my face and body with the cloth that touched the relics … St Thérèse cured me.'[6]
>
> A woman wrote: 'Directly after visiting the relics I became pregnant. This was deemed medically impossible

[6] D. Mullan, *A Gift of Roses*, Dublin: Wolfhound Press, 2001, p. 98.

for us, so I consider this a miracle. I attribute this miracle to the intercession of St Thérèse.'[7]

A newspaper account of the tour in Cork reports the reasons given by some of those present for being there. Two women are quoted as saying that they went to honour St Thérèse and to ask her to grant their requests: 'We came to leave our troubles with her and to ask her to take care of us and our families'. 'She has healed so many and can perform miracles. Hopefully she will heal some of our ailments ... We have brought petitions and roses and ask her to give us graces and bless us' (*Irish Examiner*, 21 June 2001). Reports, which I collected, of the reasons people declared for petitioning St Thérèse confirm the prominence of a desire for healing among people's requests. Taken together, the above sources suggest a demand for religious activities that recognise the potentially curative powers of prayer for the intercession of the saints. The tour of the relics of St Thérèse seemed in part to tap into that demand. The instrumental dimension found in petitioning the saint may co-exist quite comfortably with a modern society that is seen to be characterised by instrumental action. It cannot be immediately dismissed as irrational behaviour, as humans are all too aware of the limits of science when it comes to matters of health.

Nor do I believe that the tour of the relics of St Thérèse can be treated as an isolated or once-off phenomenon. There was also a high turnout for the later visit of the relics of St Anthony; another saint whom many Catholics believe can intercede to grant their petitions. Interestingly, this visit was also organised by a religious order (the Franciscans), whose own reputation, like that of the Carmelites, is largely intact. A co-ordinator of the visit, Fr Xavier Goulet, described St Anthony as 'a saint among the common people', a comment which would resonate with views expressed about St Thérèse.

[7] ibid., p. 139.

Comparisons have been drawn between the tour of the relics of St Thérèse and the papal visit in 1979. This was epitomised by the calling of the specially built van that transported the relics on the Thérèse tour, the Thérèsemobile – echoing the name of the transporter on the papal visit, the Popemobile. However, I would caution against drawing similarities, especially as regards the impact of the two visits. The papal visit took place against a background of very high levels of participation in the institutional church and high levels of confidence in the church, and in the absence of scandals. The visit became an occasion of celebration, even self-congratulation, by the Catholic Church. It was followed by a rise in the number of vocations to the priesthood. As outlined already, the context of the St Thérèse tour is very different. The attachment to the institutional church has been weakened and it is unlikely that the tour of St Thérèse's relics could substantially reverse this trend. So far there has been no evidence of a reversal in terms of attendance at Mass or in the number of vocations.

The tour of the relics of St Thérèse also allows us to comment on the relationship between the media and the Catholic Church. There has been a tendency by some Catholics, including bishops, to perceive the Irish media in recent decades as an anti-Catholic commentator and a secularising influence. The media reporting of the tour contradicts this interpretation. There was little cynicism about the tour or criticism of the Catholic Church. Perhaps journalists simply viewed the tour as an expression of popular piety. The frame of reference employed by journalists on this occasion excluded critical and negative comment about the institutional church.

There was one brief occasion of controversy during the tour. It was observed that Irish Army personnel participated in the carrying of the reliquary at Rosslare. A Protestant clergyman in Northern Ireland, the Rev. Brian Kennaway, criticised this action as indicative of excessively close ties between the state and the Catholic Church. Liberal opinion and journalists were apparently satisfied with the explanation that the armies in other countries (including Russia) had assisted with previous tours of the relics because of a traditional association between St Thérèse and the military. The participation in the tour of Irish military personnel at Rosslare was not an isolated occurrence, but was reported at some of the other Irish sites. Perhaps the fact that it did not re-ignite public debate on the issue of separation between the state and church is the surprising issue. In all likelihood, politicians recognised that the tour was popular and so were less inclined to engage in any criticism that would have cast a shadow over the events.

Conclusion

For the institutional Catholic Church, the tour of the relics of St Thérèse provided a brief interruption to the relentless reporting of scandals. It provided a temporary relief from criticism, but it has not erased the anguish or alleviated the crisis in the institutional church. The tour and the popular response do not overturn the conclusion that, in recent years, there has been a considerable increase in secularisation in modern Ireland. The tour is certainly not comparable to the papal visit over twenty years earlier and does not mark a turning point in the fortunes of the institutional Catholic Church in Ireland. The fact remains that weekly attendance at Mass has declined, confidence in the Catholic Church is low and there has been a decrease in its influence in Irish society.

However, the visit of St Thérèse's relics shows that there is a persistent popular Catholic religiosity in Ireland, which has survived both the drive towards the institutionalisation of Irish Catholicism over the preceding 150 years as well as the recent damage to the reputation of the institutional church. Some insights as to why this particular form of religion persists, while other areas of religion have declined, were obtained from accounts by participants themselves. In particular, there appears to be a considerable demand for the potentially curative powers obtained through the intercession of the saints, even in a modern, urban and well-educated society. The St Thérèse event reminds us that a distinction can be made between different dimensions of religion. Petitioning the saints may persist, as a somewhat privatised form of religious belief and practice, alongside reduced church attendance in an increasingly secular wider society.

CHAPTER 8

Digging up the Past

FARREL CORCORAN

When we look at the place of collective memory in contemporary Western societies, all the evidence seems to suggest that memory is no longer a significant social force and that it plays very little role in either private or public life. Memory studies suggest a number of reasons for this. Part of the general experience of living in an age of insistent change is that the modern present is experienced as sharply separated from the past. Youth culture often functions as a sensitive seismograph of this separation, of the rate of erosion of traditional norms, values and memory characterised by modernisation. Social theorists sometimes link this with the process of time–space compression resulting from acceleration in the felt pace of life, which shortens time horizons and expands the present. Even in the contemporary heritage industry and its culture of nostalgia, we find a revaluing of cultural memory at the far reaches of consumer capitalism, but we also find the atrophy of real history, as Frederick Jameson has suggested,[1] and the production of a feeling of 'empty time'.

What of the connections between memory and politics? This chapter argues that the assumed flattening of time and of memory across the industrialised world must be

1 F. Jameson, *Postmodernism, or the Cultural Logic of Late Capitalism*, Durham: Duke University Press, 1991.

re-examined to detect the conditions under which cultural memory plays a role in the ideological struggles that form a basis for political practice. In some societies more than others, there has always been a tendency in the political system to control cultural memory, in order to retain some influence over the shaping of the reservoir of stored meaning that is the bedrock of a political community. Attention to those special occasions where the dynamic work of memory reconstruction is intensified allows us to study an important dimension of political power, the slow formation of ideology, with all its contradictions. This chapter examines the powerful cultural reverberations of the state funeral of the 'Mountjoy Ten' in October 2001.[2] These men were IRA volunteers executed by the British government in 1920 during the War of Independence. Eight decades later, a Fianna Fáil-led Irish government decided to have the bodies removed from the prison yard where they died and reburied with full state honours in the Patriots' Plot in Glasnevin Cemetery. What did this funeral disturb in the reservoir of stored meaning associated with the foundation of the state and what role does collective memory play in the political life of contemporary Ireland?

Memory research

Academic fascination with cultural memory as an organising concept can be seen in several areas of the social sciences and humanities including sociology, media studies, literature, film studies, history, cultural studies and philosophy. This may be a reaction to what some commentators see as a weakening of modernity's faith in progress, its rejection of tradition in favour of forward-looking forgetting, and the emergence of a postmodern world of insistent immediacy and simultaneity, driven by the ubiquitous power of globalised media.

[2] The ten men were Kevin Barry, Thomas Bryan, Patrick Doyle, Frank Flood, Edmond Foley, Patrick Maher, Patrick Moran, Bernard Ryan, Thomas Traynor and Thomas Whelan.

This chapter focuses on the state–nation relationship and the problem of the ideological unity of collective memory in situations where political structures are unstable. It takes as its starting point the work of Pierre Nora, which explores the relationship between nation, identity, memory and state power, especially in political systems where 'the past' is not yet politically and historically inert and there has been little experience of institutional stability over long periods of time.[3] Of particular interest is Nora's notion of 'sites of memory', where there is a dialectical tension between a 'first-degree' understanding of original historical events, with direct person-to-person communication operating across two or three generations, and a 'second-degree' retrospective that relies heavily on the storage capacity of social institutions and media. On these sites, memories are reconstructed, revised and deployed in the production of contemporary culture. Memory sites include monuments, anniversaries, festivals, cemeteries, old prisons, sanctuaries, museum exhibitions, archives, cathedrals, places of pilgrimage, war memorials, rituals in the cult of monarchy and rituals associated with cults of the dead, including state funerals. Nora suggests that we no longer live in a world suffused with organic tradition, where memory can be sensed practically everywhere from religious ritual to culinary practices to sexual taboos.

> We speak so much of memory because there is so little of it left. The acceleration of history confronts us with the brutal realisation of the difference between real memory – social and unviolated, exemplified in but also retained as the secret of so-called primitive or archaic societies – and history, which is how our hopelessly forgetful modern societies, propelled by change, organise the past.[4]

---

[3] P. Nora, *Realms of Memory*, New York: Columbia University Press, 1998.

[4] P. Nora, 'Between Memory and History', *Representations*, vol. 26, 1989, p. 78.

This chapter considers specifically the contemporary proliferation of large-scale, spectacular events, heavily charged with symbolic meaning at their point of origin, organised by the state and displaying the awesome power of church, military and media, which create a reorganisation of the past in a struggle for the heart and soul of public opinion. Nora refers to these events as 'prosthetic memory', because of the careful deployment of external props.

The incompleteness of the decolonisation process at the centre of Irish nationalism and the persistence of a small but very active physical force tradition within that whole project, right into the twenty-first century, has generated a tension between first- and second-degree memory, and a telling of history that is deeply conflictual. Collective memory of the events of the popular uprising of 1798, or the Great Famine of 1847, or the Rising of 1916 – all recently commemorated in anniversaries as sacred events in the national tradition – is no longer passed on with one voice, its meaning intact.

In some countries, contentious differences that are integral to major turning points in a collective history (the American Civil War, the French Revolution, Cromwell's abolition of the English monarchy) lose their initial political energy and are no longer experienced as social divisions. Memory of these turning points survives into the present but in a metamorphosed form, having undergone a profound transformation into a type of cultural memory that unites rather than divides and forms the basis for political consensus. These once politically charged periods in the past are now experienced as inert cultural residues within contemporary consciousness, an amorphous temporal block, no longer politically dynamic. This is not the case with historical memory in Ireland or in other comparable countries where political institutions have not been stable for very long periods.

Irish national memory

Prosthetic memory that relies on spectacular replays of the

past in public life, politically designed to create a consensus in public opinion, can often generate further social division. This instability in prosthetic memory can be seen in the state funeral of Kevin Barry and the other nine men, drawing its emotional strength from one of the most potent rituals in the history of nationalism: the burying of the dead. This carefully orchestrated and spectacular public ritual was one of the major events in the political calendar of 2001. The bodies of ten men, executed by the British government in 1920 during the War of Independence, were disinterred from the prison yard where they had been hanged. They were reburied with full state, church and military honours in the Patriots' Plot inside Glasnevin Cemetery, itself a very significant site of memory, beside the bodies of other historical figures who had played a role in the struggle for Irish independence. The funeral cortege made a solemn, five-hour journey across Dublin, and the nation's television screens, pausing in silence or with solemn military music at significant historical sites connected with the origins of the state. Both the temporal and the spatial dimensions of this event produced a significant resonance in the Irish political system as it prepared for a general election.

The funeral was highly charged and symbolic because of the 'unfinished business' at the core of British–Irish relations, and because it was taking place against a background of dangerous instability in the newly established political institutions in Northern Ireland. By October 2001, passions on both nationalist and unionist sides in Northern Ireland were raised to higher than normal levels. The unionist parties were threatening to kill off the new political arrangement by withdrawing their consent to participate in government with their old enemies, Sinn Féin. The Northern Ireland Executive was collapsing. The Northern Ireland Assembly was locked in stalemate. The North/South Ministerial Councils were not functioning. Would the British government trigger an official review of the whole Good Friday Agreement, re-assume direct rule from London or call fresh elections? And to cap it all, the week before the state funeral, the centre of Dublin hosted a major twentieth anniversary commemoration of the death of ten IRA hunger strikers, who had challenged Margaret Thatcher's refusal to grant them political prisoner status in 1981. The past was haunting Dublin in a number of dimensions that October.

This was the potent context for the controversy that raged over a period of several weeks. Was the state funeral a long overdue, fitting mark of honour for fallen heroes? Was it a cynical move by the government to face a growing challenge from Sinn Féin and ensure its own re-election the following summer? Would this 'aggressive' gesture from the South further inflame political relationships and postpone political consensus in Northern Ireland?

The central mythic icon in this funeral drama was Kevin Barry, a 19-year-old university student and part-time IRA volunteer, arrested a few hours before he was due to resit the last of his medical examinations. His youth, his middle-class background, his nonchalant disregard for the formalities of the military court, the international campaign to save him from the gallows and his adoption as a *cause célèbre* by the influential Hearst newspaper chain across the US all guaranteed that his name in particular would survive in popular memory. The well-known ballad lamenting the execution, popularised by Paul Robeson, is still familiar to many Irish people over the age of forty. Where once a rendition of *Kevin Barry* produced a harmony of emotions – up to the 1960s at least – the memory evoked is now generating controversy, even around a theatrical depiction of Barry's execution in a regional dramatic production in Cork, with fears that touring the play in Northern Ireland would 'give offence'.

Struggle for meaning

When the government announced the date of the state funeral, opposition parties immediately pointed out that this was also the weekend of the annual Fianna Fáil convention. With massive television exposure, the government would reap a powerful public relations benefit, especially among the growing section of the electorate, many of them first-time voters, inclined to support Sinn Féin. The fact that the re-interment of the ten men with full church and state honours was taking place only six months before a general election, concentrated minds rapidly across all political parties. Opposition leaders baulked at participating in a funeral that many believed should not go ahead, least of all on the same weekend as the Fianna Fáil convention. But they could not afford to ignore this huge televised public event, timed, planned and choreographed in every detail by the government.

It quickly became apparent that there was no unanimity within the cultural memory system about the meaning of Kevin Barry in the political environment of 2001. Nationalism, as a structure of feeling originating in the nineteenth century, had seriously fragmented since the partitioning of Ireland and the long decades of the Troubles. Acceptance of the inevitability of partition had long since penetrated deeply into public consciousness as the dominant 'common-sense' viewpoint in many parts of Ireland. But the abandonment of Section 31 censorship in 1994 had released some clearly anti-partitionist voices, especially Sinn Féin's, into the public sphere.

The strongly divergent reactions to the funeral expressed this fragmentation very clearly. On one side, there was the official positioning of Kevin Barry within the mainstream consensus supporting the Good Friday Agreement. In the Requiem Mass in the Pro-Cathedral, Cardinal Cathal Daly deftly stitched together his view of the present and the past in his sermon, telling the elite congregation that the true inheritors of the ideals of the independence movement were those 'explicitly and visibly' committed to implementing all aspects of the Good Friday Agreement. He went on to warn that 'many will be laying claim to be the legitimate and only heirs of the men we reinter today ... Some will claim that the mantle has passed to them of being the men and women whose duty it is to complete the unfinished business of 1916'. The unfinished business the cardinal emphasised was not the termination of British influence in Ireland, but the building of social justice and peace.

In his graveside address, the Taoiseach stressed the democratic mandate for the use of arms by Kevin Barry, emphasising that it was grounded in the general election of 1918 and the declaration of independence issued by the Dáil in 1919. Standing in the Patriots' Plot in Glasnevin Cemetery, one of the most sacred sites in the nationalist memory system, where patriotic eulogies had been delivered throughout much of the previous two centuries, Bertie Ahern rhetorically structured his eulogy around a realisation that his national television audience would be fully aware of the existence of two other, radically opposed, ideological positions, adhered to by those who would take very different views of this funeral. One was the 'revisionist' group who would regard Kevin Barry as no more than a criminal or terrorist. The other group included those who wanted 'to stretch the democratic mandate of 1918 far beyond its natural term', that is, the Continuity and Real IRA who were continuing with the armed struggle.

Each of these viewpoints had been given expression in the media in the weeks preceding the funeral, but particularly the revisionist one because of the senior positions achieved in journalism by some of its most prominent exponents. Its crudest version was expressed in the tabloid newspaper headline 'Bury terrorism with Kevin Barry', and the attempt to associate Barry with the UVF, who had rejected the Peace Process and were continuing an ethnic cleansing policy of terrorising Catholic workers. The revisionist position argued that literally digging up the past in this way was an exercise in selective memory: why not remember also those Irishmen who had gone 'to fight for the honour of small nations' as part of the British Army in World War I? The state funeral was risking further alienation of unionists and loyalists in Northern Ireland, who would see the Barry re-interment as an exercise in atavistic republican triumphalism.

The polar opposite view to revisionism found expression too, though it had far less privileged access to the media and was generally anathematised. Among those who rejected the Good Friday Agreement, Republican Sinn Féin's President Ruairí Ó Brádaigh complained that the government had 'hijacked' the memories of the ten executed men by organising a state funeral for them, 'to calm the Irish people into believing that the British occupation of the Six Counties is normal' (*Sunday Business Post*, 9 September 2001).

Conclusion

The state funeral of Kevin Barry and his comrades clearly became an important site of memory in a period that some had already defined as post-nationalist. Many opposition politicians saw it as a clever pre-election ploy by Fianna Fáil to re-emphasise its republican credentials and see off a new electoral challenge from Sinn Féin. But it was more than this. As a five-hour television spectacle on RTÉ, and as a month-long media controversy, it rudely awakened and fully activated a cultural memory that had been relatively dormant for many years. Because of the 'unfinished business' rooted in the settlement of 1921 and fought over bitterly in the Civil War, this cultural memory had remained contentious. It was no longer a unified memory, no longer able to deliver a common interpretive framework that would support a consensual meaning for the residues that original nationalist events leave on contemporary recollection.

The state funeral does not amount to a return of the repressed in Irish culture or of a more unified sense of the nation, after a quarter century of state censorship, the Troubles and bitter revisionist polemics. But it does signify the opening up of a discursive space that had been under pressure for a long time. The funeral had no major impact on unionist opinion in Northern Ireland, despite some comments that the sweet smell of economic success south of the border had tempted the government to reclaim ground lost in the revisionist battle for ideas, symbols and memory. But it probably had a loosening effect on the institutional framework within which the struggle over meaning between different memory carrier groups takes place, particularly inside media organisations such as RTÉ.

Kevin Barry (and, metonymically, a lot of the nationalist view of the world) 'fell from grace' initially in 1989 when certain journalists began to define him not as a hero but as a vicious murderer, and to commit themselves to a revisionist reframing of republicanism as 'evil'. The state funeral can be seen as a counter-revisionist move, which will certainly alter the way we talk, or avoid talk, about 'the nation'. Whether it will yield any long-term electoral advantage to Fianna Fáil over Sinn Féin remains to be seen, though both parties secured significant increases in the general election that took place in the summer of 2002. It also remains to be seen whether it will have any impact on the embedding of Sinn Féin, newly arrived, out of belief in armed struggle and decades of censored media representation, into mainstream politics.

CHAPTER 9

Playing the Second Fiddle?

Young Men and Masculinity in Northern Ireland

DIRK SCHUBOTZ AND BILL ROLSTON

The Harland and Wolff shipyard in East Belfast has long been regarded as an icon of great significance for Ulster Protestant masculinity and identity. But all is not well behind the symbolism. Founded in 1861, the company employed 23,000 in 1950. Two decades later, the workforce was down to 9,000. The *Anvil Point*, launched in March 2003, became the last ship to be built at the once-busy shipyard. Order books are empty and less than one hundred staff are left. Harland and Wolff has been relegated to repair work on oil rigs and bridges, and shipbuilding in Belfast finally belongs to the past.

The death of shipbuilding is only the latest in a line of crises facing the Protestant male working class. For decades young men had followed the footsteps of their fathers and grandfathers and entered the factory gates of companies such as Harland and Wolff and Shorts. The decline of engineering in the 1960s, broke that pattern, but the growth of the synthetic fibres industry at the same time meant there were replacement jobs. In turn, that industry also collapsed, but the Troubles arrived just in time to provide alternative employment: at the height of the conflict, one in every eleven Protestant males was employed in 'security'.

For the Catholic working class the world of work was a very different place. The skilled engineering jobs were for the most part restricted to Protestants, the synthetic fibres factories were in mainly Protestant areas and towns, and 'security' was not a feasible career choice for any young Catholic male. Traditionally, Catholics were more likely to be unemployed, or employed in casual or less skilled work. That did not prevent them from aspiring to better opportunities, and it has been one of the successes of civil rights agitation and fair employment legislation that the labour market has become more inclusive than it once was. The irony is that just about the time when access to skilled manual jobs was made easier for Catholics, those jobs ceased to exist.

Division of labour

In Belfast, as elsewhere, men identified themselves through their work, whilst their wives were encouraged to take on the role of the mother and look after the family and the home. The concept of the male breadwinner, associated with the domestic division of labour, is a fairly recent one; it only emerged with the Industrial Revolution. It is important to note that the division of labour was an 'ideal', an aspiration rather than a clear reality. Women frequently worked outside the home, in the linen mills of Belfast for example, or the shirt factories of Derry. And men were frequently without paid employment outside the home, disproportionately so if they were Catholic. None of this prevented people, and particularly men, from aspiring to the ideal. Nor did it prevent people acting as if the ideal was a reality. Thus women who worked outside the home still had the housework to do when they came home. And men who had no work to go out to did not automatically transform themselves into househusbands. Phil Coulter's song about Derry, *The Town I Loved So Well*, portrays a town where the classic ideal was turned on its head, where women were employed in the shirt factories, 'While the men on the dole played a mother's role, fed the children and then trained the dog'. However, while the song is catchy, it is not historically correct. In reality, men's dominance over women was defined in terms of work outside the home – being or aspiring to be the breadwinner – and the avoidance of work within the home.

One effect of the domestic division of labour is that male and female sexuality came to be defined with reference to each other. Masculinity essentially became centred on the concept of breadwinner, with femininity as its opposite centred on care of the family. This polarity is captured in Best's argument that very early in life the social construct of the male identity depends on 'not being a girl' and 'not being homosexual'.[1] Later on in life, fatherhood becomes an essential element of this construction of masculinity.

This 'gender order', as Connell calls it,[2] has been starkly challenged by massive social changes, not least the restructuring of the male breadwinner role. Some old patterns remain: in Northern Ireland over twice as many men as women work full-time and men are three times more likely than women to earn over £20,000 annually. At the same time, there have been massive changes: the growth of the non-manual service sector has brought about more opportunities for jobs traditionally taken by females, girls are emerging from school with more and better qualifications than boys, and the relative success of equal opportunities legislation has meant that men are having to compete for jobs as they never had to before with young, confident, well-educated women.

The domestic scene has also changed. Beck and Beck-Gernsheim argue that the traditional Western nuclear family has become increasingly incompatible with the

1 R. Best, *We've All Got Scars*, Bloomington: Indiana University Press, 1983.

2 R. W. Connell, *Masculinities: Knowledge, Power, and Social Change*, Berkeley: University of California Press, 1995.

requirements of a rapidly changing market economy.[3] The growing number of single people is thus not a peculiar side effect of social change but is, they argue, the archetypal existence in an economy dominated by the market and technological advance. Young men, who have for generations been used to the fact that the way to the matrimonial bed led through the factory gate, are now faced with having to construct a new narrative of themselves and their own gender role.

Giddens takes the argument of the changing patterns in Western families one step further.[4] He talks of 'plastic sexuality', sexuality disconnected from reproductive behaviour. Giddens argues that, with the inevitable restructuring of family relationships, sex simply becomes a behaviour that generates pleasure or the promise of it. If sex is not primarily a reproductive behaviour, then men face challenges not only in relation to their economic activity but also in relation to the construction of the concepts of male sexuality and masculinity.

Nowhere is this more obvious than in relation to fatherhood. The introduction of the contraceptive pill revolutionised women's control over their fertility. Wives could decide not to have children if they did not want to and still fulfil what would then have been regarded as their marital duty: having sexual intercourse with their husbands. Indeed, a woman on the pill could have sexual intercourse with any man she chose in the knowledge that there was a greatly reduced risk of pregnancy. Medical advances now mean that a woman can conceive a child outside of a sexual relationship with a man. Fatherhood is effectively rendered redundant. The two key pillars which supported the traditional concept of manliness – being a father and being a worker – have collapsed.

---

3 U. Beck and E. Beck-Gernsheim, *The Normal Chaos of Love*, Cambridge: Polity Press, 1995.

4 A. Giddens, *The Transformation of Intimacy: Sexuality, Love and Eroticism in Modern Societies*, Cambridge: Polity Press, 1992.

Northern Ireland has not been immune to these seismic changes. The remarkable – in European terms – stability of traditional nuclear family patterns and attitudes has been partially dented. The 2002 Northern Ireland Life and Times survey found that over half of those asked thought it acceptable for a couple to live together without or before getting married.[5] At the same time, almost 40 per cent of both male and female respondents believed that family life suffers if a woman works full time and that what women really want is to look after the children and the home. There would thus seem to be a lag between change and people's ability to come to terms with it. This lag is particularly obvious in relation to young men in Northern Ireland.[6]

Masculinities

In Northern Ireland, as in many other places, it is a confusing time to be young and male, and it is possible to view the changes that are afoot as either a threat or an opportunity. If the decline in hegemonic definitions of masculinity is seen as a threat, the reaction is to attempt to preserve the ideal, no matter how inaccessible it was to begin with. This is the mentality behind what Faludi refers to as 'backlash'.[7] If the changes are welcomed, it will often be on the basis that there is more than one way to be a man: we can now talk of masculinities, not just masculinity. Where a young man can view a world-class footballer wearing a sarong and nail varnish, there can be a liberating redefinition of what it means to be a man. In this situation, it is not a case of a frantic search for a new masculinity to replace the old one, based on employment and dominant sexuality, but an acceptance that different men can express who they are in different ways.

5 See www.ark.ac.uk/nilt for results of the survey.

6 See K. Harland, *Young Men Talking: Voices from Belfast*, London: Youth Action and Working with Men, 1997.

7 S. Faludi, *Backlash: The Undeclared War Against Women*, London: Vintage, 1992.

The ability of young men to view the changes as an opportunity rather than a threat will depend partly on how well they have been prepared for change. So, when we undertook the first large-scale study of sexual attitudes and lifestyles of 14 to 25 year olds in Northern Ireland,[8] we were anxious not only to chart their sexual behaviour and attitudes but also to discover the extent to which young men were aware of the new challenges they face and the degree of preparation, if any, they had received from significant others such as parents, teachers and peers.

Respondents from all school sectors (Catholic, state-controlled Protestant and planned integrated, single sex, co-educational and special needs) took part in the study. Across the survey, we found that young men were less likely to receive sex education than young women. In particular, subjects that related to reproductive behaviour (such as pregnancy, menstruation or contraception) were rarely discussed with boys. As one young man said in a group discussion: boys 'are just playing second fiddle to the girls'. On the other hand, while only a minority of young people reported any coverage of non-reproductive sex (including issues such as casual sex, wet dreams, orgasm, homosexuality and bisexuality), it was young men who were more likely to report this. The fact that female sexuality is still primarily constructed around the issue of motherhood, whereas males receive less information on reproduction, reinforces the role model of the woman as the mother and person who looks after the home, while the man, at least by default, is still presumed to be the main breadwinner.

In Catholic schools this tendency was stronger than in other schools. For example, 47 per cent of young men who attended Catholic schools were not taught about menstruation, compared to only 37 per cent of males who

[8] D. Schubotz, A. Simpson and B. Rolston, *Towards Better Sexual Health: A Survey of Sexual Attitudes and Lifestyles of Young People in Northern Ireland*, London: FPA, 2002.

attended other schools. The figures for contraception are 28 and 17 per cent respectively. The existence of 'plastic sexuality' (sex without the intention to procreate) is still largely taboo in sex education in all school sectors, even if the young men are aware of such an approach to sex. To give just two examples: homosexuality was not discussed with 67 per cent of boys who attended Catholic schools and 61 per cent of boys from other schools; and sexual orgasm was never discussed with a majority of young men (65 and 53 per cent respectively in the above sectors).

There is thus endless scope for conflict between any young person at ease with the notion of sex for its own sake and a sex educator unable or unsure of how to relate to such liberal views. One 19-year-old man we interviewed graphically recounted one such conflict he had witnessed:

> ... you were never taught about masturbation, you were never taught about oral sex, all the different other types of sexual practices and you were never taught about homosexuality or all the different types of feelings and stuff. Nobody wanted really to speak about it. I remember one particular person having said: 'What is oral sex?' and the teacher just couldn't answer it. It was like: 'I have a section in a book and I'll give it to you'. And she could not tell that pupil what oral sex was. And that made him feel very embarrassed because the rest of the class was laughing at him.

In another example, a young gay man recounted his direct experience of losing out in a confrontation with teachers who were less at ease with homosexuality than he was:

> There was one class where they actually told us about a woman's womb and other things, and I turned round and said: 'How do gay people do it?'. And she said: 'You should know'. And I just looked at her and said: 'Is that a bad answer or a good answer?'. And she just looked at me and said: 'Go down to the office now'. And I went down to the

> headmaster and he said: 'What was the question you asked?'. And I said: 'How do gay people have sex?'. And he turned round and said: 'You should know'. And I said: 'Well, the teacher teaches reproduction; she should know as well'. And the headmaster said: 'Out now!' And he expelled me for three days.

It was clear from our research that the unease of teachers, as illustrated in the above two examples, could derive from any number of factors: personal belief, fear of contravening school policy, the powerful influence of religious personnel and ideologies on the management committees of most schools in the North. Whatever the reason, the effect was that in many cases, including those cited above, only one definition of masculinity was on offer.

As a result of such inadequate education, young men are unprepared for the new demands being made of them. One young father told us in an interview how difficult he found it to overcome the traditional role model in relation to his infant son:

> I mean, he is a boy, you know. And obviously there is a masculine side of things I want him to develop. I mean, I would carry him before I would push him. I would take him and walk him around the park. I wouldn't push him around the park in the pram. There has to be a bit of masculinity … I don't really worry about what other people think about me as such. I would just not push him around the park by myself in a pram.

This young man is literally caught between the past and the future – between old ideals and new ways of being a man. In as far as he and others like him can choose the future rather than the past, the old hegemonic masculinity may fade. Harland and Wolff now hosts tours for people wishing to view the place where the Titanic was built, perhaps the museum should also have an exhibit dedicated to what once used to be viewed as typical masculinity.

CHAPTER 10

Nature as Artefact on Bull Island

STEPHEN QUILLEY

Seen from the hills above the southern suburbs of Rathfarnham, Bull Island floats languidly in the grey waters of Dublin Bay – a sliver of green, drawing the eye away from the red-striped smoke stacks of the power station and the dirty bustle of the city centre towards the gentler diversions of Sutton and Howth. From this distance it has the appearance of a flat, tectonic lung – a sandy plate only just easing itself above water level, but perhaps enough to scrub clean the spirits if not the air of North Dublin. And certainly the polluted lungs and anxious minds of increasing numbers of Dubliners find cathartic relief on the island. There is psychic and spiritual balm to be found in (elusive) solitude, in physical exercise, in the fleeting experience of an uncluttered and undeveloped landscape, and the often intangible sense of engagement with nature – whether in the abrasive touch of whipped-up sea-spray, the sight of a flock of brent geese or the soothing sound of waves lapping the strand.

The experience of such inner quietude is increasingly precious in the capital. Dubliners pay the price – in traffic, pollution and stress – for miraculous but unplanned growth. For those lucky enough to have some choice about where they live, there is an unforgiving trade-off between the stress-relieving charms of more suburban and rural locations and the inescapable nightmare of commuting around a sprawling conurbation in which public transportation infrastructure compares badly with even much-maligned British cities. For many of those who cannot face commuting, or have no choice in the matter, Bull Island provides much needed respite.

The most loyal island-aficionados must be the dog walkers. Rain or shine, from early morning until after sundown, people promenade their pooches, often favouring a circular route taking in both the hillocky dunes and the long sandy strand on the seaward side. More rarely, those seeking greater solitude or perhaps a less crowded route for their ill-mannered or excitable companions, walk along the edge of the estuary on the other side of the golf course, across the mudflats of the nature reserve. Strictly speaking this is illegal, since, away from the beach, dogs are supposed to be kept on a lead to protect wildlife, particularly nesting birds. And quite frequently dog walkers attract the ire of the resident birdwatchers, who likewise favour the rain-swept days that serve to keep marauding families at bay.

I maintain a foot in both camps, being an amateur ornithologist who understands the temptation to allow his dogs to run free. Surrounded by water and devoid of interesting urban attractions such as gardens or litterbins, Bull Island is the only place in Dublin where one could allow a pair of malamute huskies off the lead without the certainty of 'incidents'. However, this latent conflict between domesticated nature (urban dogs) and wild but protected nature, is only one aspect of a multi-dimensional turf war that would be familiar to anyone charged with managing natural amenities in the vicinity of a large city.

The number of user groups that have some claim to the island is surprisingly large. Golfers using the two courses at either end of the island have secured the largest and least contested stake. The Royal Dublin is the second oldest club in the country having been founded in 1885 in Phoenix Park and then been relocated to Bull Island in 1889. Since the modern island itself only began to form after 1842, it has been landscaped, planted and ecologically dominated by the sporting priorities of the middle and upper classes for over three-quarters of its geological tenure. On sunny days, families from all over Dublin come to use the beach, parking their cars along almost the full length of the shore. When the tide is out, the hard-packed sands provide a popular venue for learner drivers and joyriders alike – the latter periodically leaving burnt-out vehicles as detritus for the tides. The strand also plays host to a range of more specialist sporting activities: windsurfers drawn to the wind-swept shallow waters of the bay, kite-fliers, and acrobatic kite-powered sand buggies taking advantage of the same conditions at low tide. And at high tide canoeists use the calmer waters of the estuary and mud flats. The undulating dunes, now firming up to host an ecological succession of shrubs and a few small trees at the centre, provide cover for young drinkers and teenage sex. And away from the unsympathetic attentions of the local gardaí, the island also provides a cottaging venue for gay men.

Bull Island as a wildlife haven

This complex ecology of sometimes competing, sometimes complementary and often mutually oblivious human activity, is largely unofficial. Aside from the golf courses, the island enters local authority discourse not in terms of the interaction of specific activities and group priorities, but as a public amenity that is, at the same time, a haven for wildlife. An area of international importance for wintering brent geese, the mudflats and salt marsh support the highest concentration of wildfowl and waders of any Irish wetland. These include sanderling, curlew, dunlin, shelduck, knot, wigeon, teal, shoveler and the usual assortment of gulls. The shallow waters are patrolled by unsightly mullets, which periodically break water with cumbersome rolls. The island itself is home to kestrels and little owls, as well as important plant species such as glasswort, sea lavender and sea aster.

Perhaps because it comes under the administrative fiat of the capital city, the island's ecological quality has received relatively high profile statutory recognition at both national and international levels. Under the Ramsar Convention ratified by Ireland in 1984, North Bull Island is designated a wetland site of international importance. It is also recognised as a biosphere reserve under the auspices of the United Nations Educational, Scientific and Cultural Organisation (UNESCO). The area has also been a designated national nature reserve since 1988.

Whilst most Dubliners are almost certainly unaware of the details of these agreements, there is a widespread understanding of the island as a nature reserve in the most general sense – an appreciation that is felt more keenly because of the obvious juxtaposition of wild nature on a site that is less than eight kilometres from the city centre. For this reason, the *idea* of Bull Island in local political discourse and public sensibility functions as a point of coalescence for anxieties and public statements about the need to protect nature more generally. For instance, in the summer of 2002 Dublin City Council, together with Coastwatch Ireland, organised a car-free day on Dollymount Strand to mark the tenth anniversary of the Rio Summit. While undoubtedly cars are a nuisance, the idea that walkers 'relished the wide open beaches without car-fumes' is a little ironic (*An Taisce*, 10 August 2002). Wind and open space generally ensure that Bull Island is the last place one would ever be aware of car fumes. Focusing on an island peripheral to the social and economic activities of Dublin, and connected to the city by only two narrow causeways rather than on central arterial routes, was hardly a convincing demonstration of commitment to the visions of sustainable development articulated at the Rio Summit.

But whilst this is perhaps indicative of gesture politics, the choice of Bull Island as the site for public anxiety is revealing. It is one small instance of a common theme in Western culture arising from the Romantic contrast between the social and urban domain of people and that of wild nature. Over the last five hundred years there has been a transformation of attitudes towards the latter, which has increasingly been seen as retreating from a rapacious and ever-advancing zone of civilisation. Nature has been problematised in terms of environmental crisis and the ecological impacts of human beings, that is, in terms of loss.

In this light the mere presence of brent geese immediately constructs Bull Island as an arena in this tug of war between 'wild nature' and 'civilisation'. Both politics and public sensibility in relation to the site are imbued with this growing sense of the sanctity of nature.[1] The ensuing structure of feeling and propriety partly explains the wrath that members of the public occasionally heap upon walkers who let their dogs off the leash around the nature reserve (this in a country where public conventions and internalised restraints in relation to littering and pooper-scooping are, for historical reasons, less advanced than in other Northern European countries). It also underlies the scorn heaped upon developers who have occasionally suggested building on this prime piece of real estate.

Geological innovation: the making of the island

As the site of a wetland, Bull Island has achieved a genuine and internationally recognised ecological significance. In more general terms, for people and politicians living in and around Dublin, it has become a symbolic touchstone for the intrinsic value of 'nature' as an objective and independent domain ever threatened by encroachment and disturbance from human activities. At the same time, as a public amenity, the island provides an arena for numerous leisure activities through which Dubliners find release from the pressures of urban life and fleeting engagement with the deeper rhythms of the natural order.

[1] The symbolic importance of this offshore, inner-city wildlife sanctuary was evident in the coverage given to a visiting white-rumped swift flying over the island on Christmas Day 2002.

When such activities are perceived to threaten what is often constructed as a natural balance and equilibrium, they become a source of tension, debate and anxiety: in small ways in relation to littering or dog-walking etiquette and in more public debates about car access, the construction of the causeway (and the silting up of the estuary) or planning permissions relating to the golf courses.

However, a moment of reflection on the history of the island reveals this equation with wild nature – little if not un-trammelled by human hands – as deeply ironic, misleading and ultimately erroneous. For a start, the entire island, and the eco-system that has grown around it, is as artificial as the coral reefs that form around the legs of deep sea oil drilling platforms: wild and emerging without directive or purposive human intervention certainly, but inherently intertwined with human activities. In this case, Bull Island itself was created as a by-product of human activity. Specifically, it was an unintended consequence of the recommendation by one Captain Bligh that the North Bull Wall should be built to prevent the accumulation of sand in the harbour. Although his survey was completed in 1800, the wall itself was finished only in 1842.

In the decades that followed, the accumulation of sand behind the wall resulted in a sandbank, which by the end of the century was durable enough for the construction of a golf course. Far from displacing natural flora and fauna, the fairways were established alongside the colonising dune grasses. It is probable that golf predates some of the island's animal and plant species and that the deliberate planting of the greens contributed to the stabilisation of the sandbanks, facilitating the wider mechanisms of ecological succession. Similarly, the extent and quality of the mudflats have varied with the nature of the bridge leading to the south end of the island and, more recently, the causeway at the north end. In more subtle ways, the categorisation of the ecosystem as a nature reserve has engendered patterns of management that have a significant impact on the plants and wildlife, from the provision of freshwater at the centre of the dune system for terrestrial species to the erection of nest boxes to encourage birds of prey.

Bull Island is a small but significant example of the transformation of a local environment as the unintended consequence of long-term processes of social development – in this case the growing importance of Dublin as a centre of commerce and the consequent expansion of the harbour facilities of the port. The construction of the Bull Wall amounted to an act of terre-formation[2] – in this case quite literally in so far as it transformed the shape of the coastline and created habitable land where there had been open water. That this land remained undeveloped for agriculture, residence or industry, serving only as a leisure amenity, ensured that relative to almost any other strip of land in Ireland, the ecological grip of human beings is relatively relaxed. It is this relaxed grip on a newly created piece of real estate that has allowed it to be requisitioned by 'wild nature' as both a new stage and a participating actor in the drama of evolutionary ecology that predates and may well postdate our own tenure in this neck of the woods. Bull Island may play host to nature – but it does so by human fiat, both in the original act of creation and in the ongoing interplay of management and regulation.

Towards a sociology of nature on Bull Island

In relation to public policy, scientific research and popular perception, Bull Island is understood very much through the categories of realist science that underpin the dominant strand of environmental sociology as well as the different strands of ecological science. Specifically the island ecosystem forms a precious natural oasis, which has been preserved from the encroachments of social development by virtue of its physical separation. This is very much the tone

2 Terre-formation is a concept that originates in science fiction, referring to the deliberate geo-biological transformation of alien worlds, rendering them habitable for human beings.

taken by the local 'interpretative centre' which rather explicitly sets out to communicate the ecological values of the site. On this basis, it is frequently identified as a rare and residual exemplar of 'nature': an objective domain, previously and potentially independent of human designs or impacts, and which can be made available to respectful human visitors through scientifically accredited 'interpretation'.

As the local historian Dennis McIntyre puts it: 'It is a natural environment set in the middle of a built up area ... accessible, large and safe ... [it is] an outdoor, living ecological laboratory'.[3] And, as McIntyre indicates, this perception of the island as a pristine ecology makes it a favourite with educationalists at all levels. Each year, over one thousand university-level students complete degrees in biological and earth sciences that have made use of Bull Island for fieldwork, long-term research and excursions. Likewise, it is a favourite with the Dublin Naturalists Field Club, the Irish Wildbird Conservancy and the Geographical Society of Ireland.

A good example of the kind of research done on the island is the project conducted by Mark McCorry and the Wetland Ecology Research Group at UCD on the effects of (and control of) spartina on a salt-marsh ecosystem.[4] The research concerns the problematic spread of a hybrid species of rhizomatous grass *spartina angelica*. Originally planted

3 D. McIntyre, *The Meadow of the Bull: A History of Clontarf*, Dublin: Shara Press, 1995.

4 M. J. McCorry and M. L. Otte, '*Spartina Angelica* at North Bull Island, Dublin. An Expanding Problem?', in H. Fuller, T. Gallagher, M. Harmey, B. Osborne and R. Otte (eds.), *Abstracts of the Irish Botanists' Meeting 1998*, Dublin: University College Dublin, 1998, p. 53. M. J. McCorry and M. L. Otte, '*Spartina Angelica*. An Aggressive Alien Invader or Beneficial New Member of Intertidal Ecosystems', in M. Downes, K. Kavanagh, C. Moriarty, D. Murray and P. Whittaker (eds.), *Abstract Royal Irish Academy, National Committee for Biology 1999 Seminar: Biological Invaders: The Impact of Exotic Species*, Dublin: Royal Irish Academy, 1999.

in the cause of coastal protection, the invasive grass is now spreading to 'areas of nature conservation value' and has been categorised as an intrusive, ecologically damaging alien. As such, on Bull Island, as elsewhere in the British Isles, *spartina angelica* has become the object of controls – a strategy initiated by ornithologists worried about the degradation of the mudflats. The object of McCorry's project is to ascertain whether the plant should be controlled and, if so, to what degree and by what means.

There should be no question, in an increasingly humanised planetary ecosystem, that if Bull Island provides a refuge for flocks of brent geese this should be duly noted and included as a priority consideration in local management strategies. Local ecosystems in which the intrusive grip of social development has been permanently relaxed by an act of legislation are always to be welcomed and defended no matter how such reserves are established and sustained. However, there are dangers in the uncritical sanctification of such areas as wilderness oases in miniature. As ecologists are increasingly beginning to recognise, human culture and social development must be included as intrinsic components of ecological models rather than sources of extraneous disturbance.

Hominids have been acting as agents of ecological transformation for millions of years. The terre-forming havoc wrought by agriculture during the last ten thousand years only escalated an existing ecological turbulence inherent in the widespread human use of fire.[5] Bull Island is the perfect example of the interaction between long-term processes of social development and the emergence of a distinctive local ecosystem. The island is a direct and recent product of human activity. The brent geese taking

5 J. Goudsblom, *Fire and Civilisation*, London: Allen Lane, 1992. S. Quilley, '"Biophilia" as a "Civilising Process": Detachment, "Secondary Involvement" and the Internalisation of Restraints in Relation to Nature', paper given to the UCD Sociology Department seminar series, January 2003.

advantage of the new terrain are intertwined with and dependent on human activity.

In the case of the geese, some of this activity comes under the label of 'ecosystem management'. McCorry's project was precisely directed at assessing the possible unintended impacts of a hybrid species of grass, propagated and planted by human beings, on bird species taking advantage of an island that is the by-product of human engineering. Put like this, the relationship between human beings, brent geese, *spartina angelica* and a sandbank they called the Bull, can be seen as a wonderful exemplar of what happens when 'nature' is redefined to include human beings and processes of social development.

In fact, scientists are increasingly moving away from the emphasis on stability, equilibrium and natural harmony that still infuses vulgar political conceptions of ecology.[6] The new ecology gives much greater recognition to chaotic, dynamic processes of change. This ties in with what Franklin sees as the beginnings of a paradigmatic shift in popular conceptions of nature.[7] In bringing ecological relationships into the foreground of politics, environmentalism is contributing to a shift away from the idea of nature as an objective and independent backdrop to human affairs – a guaranteed reservoir of resources. Nature is increasingly perceived as disordered, fragile and finite, and intimately and unpredictably intertwined with human affairs. From this perspective nature cannot be preserved from human contact and encroachment because the natural and social domains have always been inextricably intertwined.

This recognition that the nature of Bull Island is, literally, socially constructed and that human activity is a primal part of the ecological equation subtly alters the ethical and political dynamics of ecological management. Regulation cannot be aimed at maintaining or re-creating an

6 D. Botkin, *Discordant Harmonies. A New Ecology for the 21st Century*, Oxford: Oxford University Press, 1990.

7 A. Franklin, *Nature and Social Theory*, London: Sage, 2002.

autonomous and pristine nature 'as if people did not use the island'. Management becomes a more fluid and pragmatic process that necessarily involves trade-offs between different activities and interests, as well as the explicit recognition that, as the dominant species, humanity cannot avoid making strategic choices about the kind of nature we wish to conserve, create or re-create. Aesthetic and ethical priorities, as well as instrumental self-interest, will all inform the regulatory debate and there is no external 'nature' which can arbitrate.

According to Franklin, 'Nature is whatever happens to result from the interaction between species including the actions and designs of man; it is a result of history unfolding; it is the outcome of "co-dwelling" … it is local'.[8] This is a useful point of departure for a sociological investigation of Bull Island that would seek to reconstruct the unfolding task and activity-scapes through which social and natural processes have co-constructed the geological and ecological landscape of the island over the last one hundred and fifty years. Such an account would focus on the interaction between local processes of social development on the one hand – the construction of the Bull Wall, the establishment of golf courses, the designation of nature reserves, the scientific investigation of the island ecosystem, the creation of an interpretative centre, the construction of a causeway and car-parking facilities etc. – and geo-ecological processes on the other – the formation of a sandbank, colonisation by dune grasses, silting up of the former Dollymount shoreline to create a system of mudflats, the invasion by wading birds, colonisation by the alien hybrid *spartina angelica* etc.

However, the fact that human activity has, in this case, actually created an island and reconstructed the Dublin coastline points also to a longer timeframe, which is possibly more illuminating. The ten to twelve thousand years since the last Ice Age have witnessed the process of

8 ibid., p. 9.

agrarianisation and the escalating trajectory of social development that turned humanity into a significant geological, morphological and ecological agent of change. Among earth scientists, there has been a growing appreciation of the weight and influence of human activities on global ecology. In particular, much has been made of the qualitative acceleration in human impacts since the eighteenth century.

Two key ideas underpin our contemporary understanding of the relationship between social development and the biosphere. First, there is no fixed, harmonious natural equilibrium for human beings to upset. Ecological, geological and climatological processes interact over different timeframes in incredibly complex ways, switching from benign periods of stability to moments of climactic upheaval with frightening rapidity. And second, human beings are part of nature. Processes of social development are now changing our world to such an extent that we may be complicit in triggering or contributing to such an upheaval.[9] From a sociological perspective, the emphasis on process is valuable in so far as it points to the long-term iterative relationship between social development and ecological regimes. Assuming that humanity is able to survive, it seems certain that in the future the trajectory of natural ecosystems and planetary ecology will become increasingly managed and directed in the context of a system of global ecological management. Failure in this venture will not spell the end of nature, but it will probably mean extinction or catastrophic implosion of human civilisation.

Bull Island is an instructive microcosm of these dilemmas: the meaning and management of autonomous nature and its relation to wider social and economic processes. As a geological innovation, the island itself is a

[9] C. Tudge, *The Time Before History. Five Million Years of Human Impact*, New York: Touchstone, 1997.

transformation that could last tens of thousands of years. The mudflats ecosystem may be dependent on the ongoing negotiation between the immediate priorities of social and economic development and our long-term dependence on natural systems. In a small way, if we can be clear about whether *spartina angelica* is an undesirable, invasive alien, or rather one local example of the result of interaction between species, then we will be a long way towards understanding the wider relationship between humanity and nature.

PART 3

GOING PLACES

Peripheral height

Brandcentral

Spire and GPO by Conor Caffrey, 2004

Community art, St Michael's estate, Dublin

CHAPTER 11

Selling Regional Identity: The Case of Fuchsia Brands Ltd

ETHEL CROWLEY

In this era of global consumerism, those in business have to do everything possible to gain an edge over their competitors. This includes attaching symbols of 'quality' to foods and services from particular regions. This chapter looks at the entrepreneurial construction of West Cork by Fuchsia Brands Ltd. This regional branding initiative aims to distinguish food products and tourist-related services from the West Cork region as quality items that will satisfy the more discerning consumer. This approach has already been used in other regions of Europe and in the US.

The global and the local

Social life is influenced by inputs from several levels, ranging from that of the global to the personal and including EU, national, regional and local levels. All of these interconnect, and not necessarily in a top-down direction. A rural region like West Cork can be experienced as both local (with its connotations of home, roots and other emotional connections) and cosmopolitan (satisfying the need for exposure to wider economic and cultural influences) simultaneously. No longer does one have to make a stark choice between town and country. Developments in telecommunications have resulted in more links between the people of West Cork and the wider world, but that does not necessarily mean that they are any less linked to their home. Many people in West Cork, and elsewhere, have developed lifestyles that easily combine those activities commonly associated with globalisation (like working for a multinational or using the Internet) with others that evoke the local (like playing in the local women's football team) without incongruity.

The essential qualities of a place depend upon whose ideas about the present and future of that place become dominant at any particular time. Massey insists that the places in which people live are shaped by these power struggles, and that 'localities are constructions out of the intersections and interactions of concrete social relations and social processes in a situation of co-presence'.[1] If a place is defined by its inhabitants, then it cannot be understood in just one way, but must necessarily be viewed from various perspectives. Whelan, for example, suggests that the county in Ireland, which has been so literally played upon by the Gaelic Athletic Association, is in fact a very arbitrary division that represents, for him, 'the successful imposition of the English shiring system'.[2]

The people that inhabit a place may represent interests, or clusters of interests, that stretch beyond the physical boundaries of place. Local people and their associates dispersed beyond the locality embody a rich variety of cultural, economic, social and political perspectives. Hence an area such as West Cork, composed of complex and varied physical realities and different sets of individuals, engenders a diversity of meaning-clusters.

1 D. Massey, *Space, Place and Gender*, Cambridge: Polity Press, 1994, p. 138.

2 K. Whelan, 'The Bases of Regionalism', in P. Ó Drisceoil (ed.), *Culture in Ireland: Regions: Identity and Power*, Belfast: Institute of Irish Studies, Queen's University Belfast, 1993, p. 10.

One such meaning-cluster is that dominated by rural development 'experts'. The main vehicle for funding Fuchsia Brands Ltd has been the EU, through the LEADER programme. One of LEADER's aims is to initiate bottom-up development by building and facilitating links between local entrepreneurs. LEADER I ran from 1991 to 1994, LEADER II from 1994 to 1999, and LEADER + began in 2000 and is scheduled to run until 2006. It has been seen as a means of encouraging local initiative and reducing dependence on the state. However, a number of critiques have been levelled at LEADER. For instance, it is argued that it is usually the better-off members of society who benefit most from LEADER funding, while the majority of rural-dwellers remain unaffected.[3] Furthermore, 'empowering' local communities to provide services for themselves has been described as a cost-cutting exercise, with local volunteers becoming 'a source of cheap or free labour'.[4] Finally, it tends to professionalise local development and incorporate local initiatives into a supra-national bureaucratic framework.[5]

There seems to be a suspicion among some commentators that LEADER tends to promise more than it actually delivers in terms of consolidating local development strategies and creating employment for those who need it most. Chris Eipper, in his seminal study of power relations in Bantry,[6] found that a small cadre of influential people dominated local community life, and it now appears that LEADER works in more or less the same way. Nevertheless, the LEADER programme has helped to underwrite

---

3 D. Storey, 'Issues of Integration, Participation and Empowerment in Rural Development: The Case of LEADER in the Republic of Ireland', *Journal of Rural Studies*, vol. 15, no. 3, 1999, p. 313.

4 S. Martin, 'Democratising Rural Development', in N. Walford, J. Everitt and D. Napton (eds.), *Reshaping the Countryside: Perceptions and Processes of Rural Change*, London: CAB International, 1999, p. 177.

5 D. Storey, 1999, op. cit., p. 314.

6 C. Eipper, *The Ruling Trinity: A Community Study of Church, State and Business in Ireland*, Aldershot: Gower, 1986, p. 134.

entrepreneurial initiatives in West Cork and, in particular, the development of a branding strategy.

Reinventing the region

Before considering the case of Fuchsia Brands Ltd, let us examine new ways of attaching meaning to regions. Because of various trends associated with globalisation, the main unit of analysis for social scientists can no longer be presumed to be the state. Many contemporary economic, political and cultural developments are no longer dependent upon the state and there is ample evidence of the increasing inter-penetration of global and local levels. The more pressure that is exerted by powerful economic and cultural forces, the more people may yearn to emphasise their local identity and stress their difference to the sameness being imposed from outside. People may need a human-scale frame of reference, to complement the broader global context.

This is demonstrated by a new form of regionalism that has been grasped by entrepreneurs in some regions of the Western world, and is especially visible in the realm of food and tourism marketing. New concerns about food safety and the increasing sophistication of the taste buds of a large portion of the population have led to the creation of a market for many new and varied products. The desire for reliable quality food is inherently a product of globalisation: it is a reaction to the poor quality of mass-produced food, the manufacture and sale of which is increasingly controlled by just a few global corporations. However, the production of niche-market foods will never supersede more conventional food production, as poorer people will continue to eat the cheaper, mass-produced, highly processed foods. Nevertheless, niche marketing is a significant phenomenon, whether it is associated with organics, animal welfare or local produce.

One aspect of this trend is the attachment of regional identities to some food products in an attempt to confer a sense of authenticity upon them, and hence add value. Regions are packaged anew for the consumer and imbued with symbolic significance. Regional food 'traditions' are created and capitalised upon, and situations arise where 'regional identity becomes enshrined in bottles of wine or hunks of cheese'.[7] Some gastronomic regions do indeed have a long-established cultural history and are associated with definite local products, such as fish dishes from Brittany, fruit-based products from Alsace and dairy products from Normandy. Others are more recent creations, like the French wine-producing regions, where the designation of *appellation d'origine* was controlled by powerful political actors when it was legally established in 1935.

Given the various food scares experienced in Western consumer societies in recent years, the politics of food has become more sensitive, and indeed potentially explosive. Some producers have the skills and ability to circumvent, or even profit from, the fears that have been generated in relation to BSE, E.coli and foot and mouth disease. The representation of some foods as 'quality foods' is one important means of achieving competitive advantage. This approach has been sanctioned by the EU in Regulations 2081/92 and 2082/92, which set down the rules for protecting food and drink products that have a special character or a recognisable geographical origin. The regulation of 'quality' has become a very politicised arena.

Reinventing West Cork

Fuchsia Brands Ltd is a regional branding initiative, based in West Cork, which attempts to confer a quality label upon its products. Before discussing the brand, let us take a brief look at the region itself. There are a number of ways that West Cork may be viewed: a cosy rural getaway, a place of economic decline or a locale ripe for investment. It is an area

7 D. Bell and G. Valentine, *Consuming Geographies: We are Where we Eat*, London: Routledge, 1997, p. 148.

undergoing rapid change: it never had a strong industrial base, but farming is on the wane and tourism is increasing in importance economically and changing the social character of the place in numerous ways. West Cork these days is recognised for its world-renowned bird observatory at Cape Clear, the haunting melodies of composer Seán Ó Riada and as the home of writers Somerville and Ross. Most Irish people would associate it with an easy pace of life, friendly inhabitants, a clean environment, beautiful rugged scenery, music festivals and Babel-like pubs.

West Cork is an area of demographic ebbs and flows. It has strong affinities with other places on the globe, these being the destinations of emigrants and the original homes of immigrants. Places like the Bronx in New York and Camden Town in London, with large clusters of Irish emigrants, are very much part of West Cork's world and are co-ordinates on West Cork people's mental maps. The area has a reputation for a relatively high level of in-migration, in the form of both Irish and foreign-born new residents, second-home owners, retirees from Continental Europe and New Age travellers. These in-comers choose the more robust lifestyle of the West Cork countryside, rejecting the conveniences of urban life. It is probably the case that the members of this group derive primarily from the middle class and upper middle class in their places of origin. They have a more conscious sense of cultural association, since they have no family roots in the area upon which they can rely for identity. They are self-contradictory in a way: because while they may be cosmopolitan in their outlook, they are still searching for an organic community in the area. This social mix of locals and in-comers has created a particularly dynamic environment for business innovation.

Fuchsia Brands Ltd

As already mentioned, one of the most popular images of the region is that of beautiful scenery and a clean and unspoilt environment. This is now being capitalised upon by Fuchsia

Brands Ltd, a recent innovation which markets West Cork tourist enterprises and food products under its own indigenous brand. Both of these sectors could be seen as dependent on regional identity. The logo used – an image of the red and purple fuchsia flower – is intended to be reminiscent of the small, pretty country roads in which the fuchsia bushes flourish. The image used on the promotional literature as the backdrop to the food display, that of an idyllic farmhouse perched on a dramatic cliff overlooking a cobalt blue sea, is actually a computer-generated montage and does not exist in reality. The aim is that the fuchsia would become symbolic of high quality, clean, rural-based foods and services. The fuchsia logo takes two forms: for tourism, it is surrounded by the words 'A Place Apart – West Cork', and for food: 'A Taste of West Cork'.

Initiated in February 1998, this limited company comprises representatives from West Cork LEADER, West Cork Food Producers' Association and Cork/Kerry Tourism, and was developed with inputs from the EU, food economists and tourism interests. The project is supported by significant investment by selected private companies, especially in marketing and tailored quality training programmes. The EU provides 50 per cent of funding for the initiative, based as it is on the principle of matched funding. It received almost half of all funding supplied by LEADER II in West Cork. The project is an attempt to gain competitive advantage, in the words of the chief executive officer of Fuchsia Brands Ltd, by 'turning around peripherality'. Using this strategy, West Cork is marketed by LEADER as an entrepreneurial seedbed and a potentially prime site for new investment.

Due to economic pressures in recent years, West Cork has been very consciously re-inventing itself as an important tourist centre. This coincides nicely with the most potent image in EU rural development policy, that of the 'multifunctional countryside' dedicated to the 'production of renewable raw material for non-food purposes or the energy sector, rural tourism, marketing of high-quality produce or the preservation of our cultural heritage'.[8] The agricultural policy that was largely responsible for substantial rural depopulation is now repackaging the countryside as a tourist-friendly, sanitised version of itself. This means that 'the local sense of place is being replaced by an outsider's view of what is significant in the locality, i.e. the outsider's sense of place'.[9] This approach to development may also be found to exclude those local inhabitants who are outside of the entrepreneurial milieu in whose interests it is to foster this ethos.

Small tourist enterprises, ranging from self-catering cottages to pitch-and-putt courses to Japanese restaurants, have developed all over the area. It is estimated that the equivalent of 1,200 full-time jobs are dependent on tourism, and jobs have been created in extremely peripheral areas where little or no other employment exists. West Cork, however, is vulnerable to a number of factors, such as a high level of seasonality, labour shortages, its distance from the Dublin area and increasing competition from other regions. The jobs created in tourism are often low grade, low paid, seasonal and unreliable in character. Female job ghettos are created in this sector, serving only as stopgap (usually summer only) employment for Ireland's increasingly well-educated young workforce. Many catering establishments are now turning to foreign labour, because few young Irish people are willing to work for the relatively low wages that are usually paid. The treatment of some immigrant workers in such establishments will no doubt become an issue in years to come. So far, however, they are in too weak a position to bargain with some unscrupulous employers.

The second branch of Fuchsia is the production of high quality, niche-market, artisanal food products, the ingredients of which are sourced locally. These products

[8] F. Fischler, 'CAP 2000 – A Framework for the Future of EU Agriculture', *Farmer's Journal*, 6 September 1997, p. 36.

[9] E. Slater, 'Cast a Cold Eye: Packaging Irish Heritage', *Irish Reporter*, vol. 10, second quarter, 1993, p. 10.

include yoghurt, milk, butter, eggs, honey, jams, herbs, smoked fish, shellfish, cakes, desserts and cheeses like Durrus, Gabriel, Gubbeen and Milleens. These enterprises are owned by locals, and sometimes by in-comers to the area. The latter have made a major contribution to the development of a local food culture. The chief executive officer of Fuchsia Brands feels that the multiculturalism of this sector is an asset to be celebrated and encouraged and that it is part of the distinctiveness of West Cork. These entrepreneurial in-comers contribute to the local economy by providing employment. Also, many of the gourmet products are quite exotic in Irish terms, and could by no means be described as native to the region or part of a distinctive regional cuisine. High quality cheese was never part of the Irish diet until it was more or less introduced by German, Dutch and English in-comers towards the end of the twentieth century. Indeed, much innovation is in evidence, embodied in products such as chowder, salsa, duck and cheesecake.

The food initiative is an example of a type of economic development that, on the one hand, builds upon a local resource base and labour market and, on the other, is geared towards the international consumer. Its promotional literature reminds us that 'west Cork's renown as a place of culinary excellence, artistic expression and quality endeavour, reflect positive local characteristics such as environmental quality as well as the richness and diversity of its landscape, heritage and tradition'. The strong symbolic power that Fuchsia products possess ensures that they have a good chance of success at a time when homogenisation of food products and declining standards in food production have become important public issues. Capitalising on the idea of authenticity is an opportunistic marketing strategy that has often been associated with Italy, and most famously with Parmesan cheese. More recently, Italy has become the launching pad for the slow food movement. Now more than ever, it is in entrepreneurs' interests to re-value local characteristics as EU policymakers recognise the high consumer demand for the non-homogenised, locally based, handmade product. LEADER's positive view of the Fuchsia branding initiative is expressed thus on its website: 'The keys to the success of this initiative are its use of a genuine sense of regional identity and the integrated nature of the supports delivered to stimulate enterprise and community activity'.[10]

Jaap Frouws, in a different light, views this type of development strategy as part of what he terms the 'hedonist discourse', a view of the countryside which originated from the urban elite. He argues that the rhetoric of rural renewal, landscapes of quality and relocalisation serves a deeper structural function: 'as a pretext and a licence, under the aegis of contemporary neo-liberalism, for the on-going scale enlargement and industrialisation of agriculture as well as the relentless activities of property developers looking for investment opportunities, which tend to suffocate the very process of renewing the countryside'.[11] While views on this will inevitably differ, the likelihood remains that this strategy, and its equivalents elsewhere, will be supported by the EU for many years to come.

Conclusion

Using the image of a fuchsia as a marketing tool, rural development professionals and business interests in West Cork have packaged some elements of the local countryside in an attempt to persuade consumers to purchase goods and services produced in the region. In doing so, they are capitalising upon a contrived sense of authenticity. The entrepreneurial construction of West Cork is a largely

[10] www.westcorkleader.ie. I would like to acknowledge the kind assistance of Seamus O'Reilly, Department of Food Economics, UCC, in conducting this research.

[11] J. Frouws, 'The Contested Redefinition of the Countryside. An Analysis of Rural Discourses in the Netherlands', *Sociologia Ruralis*, vol. 38, no. 1, 1998, p. 64.

artificial one and, as a result, its overall impact is likely to be limited. The Fuchsia brand has been grafted onto the products of an already-established entrepreneurial milieu in the region. It will probably enhance the survival chances of those who are least at risk of marginalisation, but it will have little impact on the deeper social problems that exist in the region, related to poverty, exclusion and isolation.

CHAPTER 12

Place Re-Making in Dublin

MARY P. CORCORAN

One of the defining features of the city of Dublin in recent years has been its diffusion into the surrounding hinterland, creating major outlying suburban communities some of which now qualify as 'edge cities'. One consequence of this diffusion is a re-orientation of the citizenry away from the downtown. It is hard to imagine now but, in the 1940s and 1950s, O'Connell Street was the vibrant core of the city of Dublin replete with entertainment, restaurant, hotel and business facilities. If we try to think of an iconic image from that period, it has to be that of young men and women, sensibly belted against the wind and rain, waiting expectantly for their dates under Clerys' clock. From the 1960s, as the commercial heart of the city migrated across the River Liffey to Grafton Street and St Stephen's Green, O'Connell Street and its surrounding environs went into decline. While the city centre's main thoroughfare retained its status as the civic centrepoint – it is still the main route for all protest marches in the city – lax planning laws saw it increasingly colonised by burger joints, gaming arcades and pound shops. The sad decline of O'Connell Street served to deepen the northside/southside distinction already embedded in the city's narrative.

By the late 1990s, Dublin City Council (then called Dublin Corporation) had devised a bold strategy for visually refashioning O'Connell Street, and restoring the thoroughfare to its former glory. Central to this strategy was the commissioning of a millennium monument to be erected on the former site of Nelson's Pillar. Throughout 2001 and 2002, Dublin City Council, the general public, the business community on O'Connell Street, artists and environmentalists publicly debated the merits of the chosen design, the 'Spire of Dublin'. While it is clear that part of the agenda is to make the street economically viable once again, there is a wider reasoning behind the municipality's plan of aestheticisation. Cultural objects are more than simply aesthetic, they are part of the symbolic economy which 'constructs both a currency of commercial exchange and a language of social identity'.[1] The Spire represents a vehicle both for the economic revalorisation of the northern side of the river and the expression of a new kind of national and urban narrative. Furthermore, it constitutes a key artefact in the attempted transformation of the spatial order of the city.

Re-orienting urban renewal in Dublin

The evolution of the built environment, whether in the urban core, on the edge of the city or in the outer suburbs, takes place in a political and economic context. Changes have been wrought by the impact of economic global forces working themselves out on local urban landscapes. Urban planning processes have become dominated by the objective of positioning the inner city as an object of inward investment. There is ample evidence that this has been the case in Dublin.

The impetus for urban regeneration in the city was provided by the Urban Renewal Act, 1986, which made available a generous package of tax-based incentives to

[1] S. Zukin, 'Space and Symbols in an Age of Decline', in A. King (ed.), *Re-presenting the City*, London: Routledge, 1998, p. 45.

developers, investors and owner-occupiers. In response to this scheme, and given the generally more favourable prevailing economic circumstances, Dublin in the 1990s experienced a building boom in the office and commercial sectors. The state effectively acted as a catalyst for commercial development and, at the same time, ensured a market for what was actually built through the additional tax incentives for occupancy of commercial buildings and private dwellings. More significantly though, the Act set the context for a re-imagining of Dublin, which altered the vernacular of the city over the decade that followed, in particular through flagship development projects such as the International Financial Services Centre and the cultural quarter of Temple Bar. Provincial Dublin was consigned to the past, to be replaced by gleaming new office blocks, riverside apartment developments, a new restaurant culture and the super pub.

Integrated area planning

More recently, Dublin City Council has attempted a re-crafting of its urban renewal programme to incorporate a 'public good' dimension alongside the more overtly economic motivation that had hitherto dominated. While the original urban renewal scheme developed in 1986 was generally deemed successful, it has been widely accepted that the scheme did little to enhance the socio-economic opportunities of indigenous urban communities. The need for an integrated planning approach was highlighted and subsequently translated into the Department of the Environment's *Guidelines for Integrated Area Plans* (1997), and the Council's *Dublin City Development Plan* (1999). The government approved a new urban renewal scheme in 1998, which provided for a more planned, integrated and focused approach to urban renewal designations. Relevant local authorities seeking designation were required to prepare integrated area plans (IAPs) for parts of urban areas in most need of physical and socio-economic rejuvenation.

O'Connell Street plaza, Dublin City Council

The core objective of the IAP drafted for O'Connell Street is to alter the character of the public domain of the street and its environs through a combination of cultural and aesthetic projects and the tax designation of specific sites. This approach is predicated on the view that economic engines underpin local areas, but equally important are local cultural clusters. The idea underlying the IAP is to stimulate both the economy and culture of the neighbourhood, to re-animate the city centre and to re-invigorate its civic character. According to the IAP:

> … nothing short of a redefinition of the existing uses is necessary if the street is to become effective as the main street of the capital and of the country. This will involve the development of a range of uses that generate animation, vitality and the kind of atmosphere that draws all sectors of society into the street and makes people want to stay.[2]

2 www.dublincity.ie/dublin/oconniap2.html

Rather than the street being simply a place that is passed through, the plan envisions a street that people will choose to visit. But to do this, O'Connell Street has to have its sense of place restored.

The Spire and place-remaking in Dublin

As part of the overall strategy for the improvement of O'Connell Street, Dublin City Council advanced a proposal to construct a new monument at the site of the former Nelson's Pillar, to be chosen by way of an international competition. The winning entry – 'Monument of Light' by Ian Ritchie Architects, London – was announced in 1998. The stainless steel monument is a conical spire that tapers from a diameter of 3 metres at the base to a 0.1 metre pointed pinnacle at a height of 120 metres. Initial work on the monument was delayed by Judicial Review proceedings, which sought an environmental impact statement for the project. The statement was duly prepared and certified by the minister. Work began on building the Spire in 2001 and was largely completed by the end of 2002. This was followed by the second part of Phase 1 of the O'Connell Street redevelopment programme, which involves the construction of a paved granite plaza from the Spire to the General Post Office, lined with clipped lime trees and lit by four 16-metre-high lighting masts.

Cultural politics and politico-economic power inevitably become intertwined in the social process of place construction or re-construction. The 'Monument of Light', later renamed the 'Spire of Dublin', is intended to celebrate and become symbolic of the re-invention of O'Connell Street. The tawdry provincialism of the street will be refashioned into a European-style boulevard of the twenty-first century. The creation of the Spire in O'Connell Street, however, is about more than the aestheticisation of the street, although that is central to its brief. It is also about revalorising the street as an economic entity. The development of the Spire cannot be divorced from the expensive makeover of Clerys department store, the introduction of planning laws to make it more difficult to open 'low-end' outlets on the street and the proposed re-development of the former Carlton cinema site. Indeed Dublin City Council's vision is to re-create O'Connell Street as a quality environment with a range of higher-end uses. It is hoped that the Spire will draw people across the river, providing a beacon of the regeneration of the north inner city and a landmark to orient the local and visiting *flâneur*.

Public monuments, street names, urban planning and architectural initiatives are fundamentally spatial phenomena, rooted in the domain of the cultural landscape.[3] Building on the insights of Lefebvre, Harvey contends that 'the material practices and experiences entailed in the construction and experiential qualities of place must be dialectically interrelated with the way places are both represented and imagined'.[4] We can think about the Spire in terms of these three dimensions: the materiality of place, its representation and its place in the imagination.

O'Connell Street is a distinct cultural space, with its own specific history and determinants. In the eighteenth century, O'Connell Street (formerly Sackville Mall) was originally intended as an elongated residential square rather than a busy commercial thoroughfare.[5] By the early nineteenth century, the street had become a prestigious commercial boulevard complete with shops, hotels and businesses, predating the similar development of great city-centre avenues in London and Paris. During the Rising in 1916, three-quarters of the buildings on the street were destroyed. The re-building of O'Connell Street became a major concern in the immediate aftermath of the Rising and

3 Y. Whelan, *Re-inventing Modern Dublin*, Dublin: University College Dublin Press, 2003, p. 234.

4 D. Harvey, 'From Place to Space and Back Again', in J. Bird et al. (eds.), *Mapping the Future: Local Cultures, Global Change*, London: Routledge, 1993, p. 17.

5 www.dublincity.ie/profile/publications/iap/oconnellfullaca.pdf

strict guidelines governing height, proportions and corners were implemented in a bid to retain the character of the street. In the 1940s and the 1950s, the street was at the height of its popularity, playing a key commercial, cultural and civic role at the heart of the city.

Clerys' clock

The spatial reorganisation of the city since the 1960s has not been kind to O'Connell Street. Uneven capitalist development in Dublin helped to produce the material decline of the street and its environs, as commercial development moved south of the river or out of the city altogether. The street became characterised by fast food shops, games arcades and vacant lots (a building next to the Carlton cinema site, for example, has been vacant since 1979). In terms of its representation, the street became defined predominantly by its marginality to the city's economy and culture despite its central location. Dubliners increasingly viewed it with foreboding (a 'no-go' area was a popular designation) or indifference. Sited in the unfashionable quarter of the city, O'Connell Street soon became a leitmotif for all that we dislike about the urban condition – drab, dangerous, run down, and virtually deserted at night.

As the city of Dublin has become increasingly subordinated to the capitalist marketplace, there is increasing pressure to counteract placelessness by differentiating spaces within the urban landscape and celebrating them symbolically. Dublin City Council's re-imagining of the city, which is given expression in the *Dublin City Development Plan*, the integrated area plans and in the City Development Board's strategy, *Dublin: A City of Possibilities*,[6] attempts to revalorise the city through a new focus on place, identity and neighbourhood. This interweaving of economy and culture is key to the setting of objectives for particular places in the city:

> The vision for O'Connell Street must include a broad-based commitment to create the kind of quality environment, range of uses and powerful sense of place that can live up to its unequivocal role as the main street

6 Dublin City Development Board, *Dublin 2002-2012, A City of Possibilities, Economic, Social and Cultural Strategy*, Dublin: Dublin City Development Board, 2002.

> of the capital city; a street where there is a strong dynamic relationship between quality architecture and a vibrant mix of uses, and where a co-ordinated design approach to the public domain is balanced by a concern to develop the social and cultural dimensions of the public spaces; a place where people are attracted to, and feel both stimulated and secure by day and night.[7]

While acknowledging the significance of economic engines of regeneration, Dublin City Council seeks to promote the cultural and civic character of Dublin's neighbourhoods. As an acknowledgement on the part of the municipality that place matters, this represents a significant development. In the wake of the first Spencer Dock planning debacle, a long overdue attempt has been made to articulate a coherent vision for the city of Dublin. The Council is responding to the fear of placelessness, associated with the erosion of a public moral sphere in favour of privatised consumption and tourism. This entails the adoption of a clear political position, wherein culture is promoted as 'a point of concern' underscoring the decision to invest (even in the face of public criticism) in a new symbol for O'Connell Street. That symbol can then be appropriated instrumentally to achieve cultural, political and economic ends.

The Spire is more than a cultural or aesthetic intervention on the street. It is there to safeguard the viability of current and future commercial space. Clerys department store has undergone a multi-million euro makeover and plans are now advanced for a major redevelopment of the Carlton site. The business community has been vocal in its support for the Spire, because of the potential spin-off economic benefits for the street. In a letter to *The Irish Times* on 15 January 2001, the Chairman of Best Ltd, a family-owned company that has traded on the street for more than fifty years, commented: 'we are very conscious

7 A. Graham, *O'Connell Street Integrated Area Plan, Annual Report 2000-2001*, Dublin: Dublin City Council, 2001, p. 2.

that the street has suffered during the years since the departure of the Nelson monument. Accordingly, we thoroughly approve of the decision to replace Nelson with a landmark monument worthy of the capital of our country'.

The attempt to bring the rejuvenation to fruition has neither been smooth nor straightforward. The execution of the plan for O'Connell Street alerts us to some of the tensions and ambiguities that exist between the stated goals for the street and how they can be achieved in practice. For example, much of the rhetoric of Dublin City Council focuses on O'Connell Street as a civic space, with the Spire and the new GPO plaza providing a pedestrian-friendly focal point at the south end of the street. Yet, at the same time that plans were moving ahead for the Spire, the Council sought (unsuccessfully) to ban protest marches from O'Connell Street. Had the Council succeeded this would have negated the whole notion of the street as a particular kind of public sphere lending itself to mass gatherings and symbolic speech-making in front of the GPO.

Similarly, the democratic idea of creating high quality civic space at the centre of the city sits rather uncomfortably with the need to ensure that the city is safe for visitors and citizens alike. A major multi-agency initiative launched in 2003 targeted littering, vandalism and other anti-social behaviour in an effort to create a safer, cleaner environment in Dublin's main business and shopping zone, described by the Dublin City Manager, John Fitzgerald, as 'the front parlour' of the city (*The Irish Times*, 22 October 2003). Under the initiative, thousands of people on the city streets were arrested, and begging and street drinking in the city centre have been almost fully eradicated as a result. The streets, in effect, have been cleared of those members of the public who are deemed 'undesirable', in order to make them more attractive to everyone else.

A third tension emerged in relation to the vernacular element of the streetscape. The original plans for the street clearly indicate that most of the plane trees on the central median would be replaced with smaller, European-style trees and manicured hedging. But when the offending specimens were being unceremoniously felled, a number of Green Party politicians dramatically chained themselves to the trees, and Dublin City Council received hundreds of email and telephone complaints from the general public. After a flurry of public debate, some of the trees were subsequently given a stay of execution. Apart from their historic role as 'witnesses' to the 1916 Rising, the trees also formed part of a natural habitat for wagtails. The reluctance on the part of the public to accept the demise of the trees signals a certain ambiguity about the terrain of O'Connell Street. On the one hand, the idea of re-modelling the street along the lines of a European boulevard is welcomed as an example of Ireland's 'coming of age'. On the other hand, people retain concerns about sweeping change that threatens to obliterate memory, history and heritage on O'Connell Street.

These tensions suggest that the question as to whether or not 'the public' can be successfully re-claimed on O'Connell Street remains. And, more pertinently, we might ask to what does 'the public' actually refer, particularly in the context of conflicting policies that seek to re-animate civic space while simultaneously clearing that space of those deemed undesirable. This has prompted some cultural critics to question whether there is 'any such thing as a public sphere in the culture of late capitalism'.[8]

Inspiring imagination

The evaluation and hierarchical ranking of places – both within cities and between different cities – occurs largely through activities of representation. It is possible to think about O'Connell Street as a space of representation that has over time played a significant role in how Irish people imagine their capital city, the country and themselves.

8 W. J. T. Mitchell (ed.), *Art and the Public Sphere*, Chicago: University of Chicago Press, 1992, p. 2.

The Spire of Dublin

Despite its material decline it has continued to exercise a distinctive hold on the public imagination. The buildings and monuments on O'Connell Street speak of legendary heroes – Daniel O'Connell, Charles Stuart Parnell, James Larkin and the popular movements that they led: Catholic emancipation, national self-determination and the labour movement, respectively. The street also evokes memories of the Rising, of the blowing up of Nelson's Pillar, of wet St Patrick's Day parades, of soccer team homecomings and of political marches. Now, the street (and the city centre) is being re-imagined.

A main attraction of the Spire is its iconic potential. While it has only been in place for a short time, it is well on its way to occupying a symbolic place in contemporary culture. One of the early battles that had to be fought by Dublin City Council was to get control of the Spire's potentially lucrative Internet domain name. The Dublin City Development Board has made the Spire a central element of its logo. Two recently published books use the Spire to great effect on their front covers.[9] RTÉ Television features the Spire on its promotional inserts between programmes. The Spire represents a vehicle through which we might dream of new urban futures. In fact, Ian Ritchie has described it as 'symbolising growth, search, release, thrust ... a pure symbol of optimism for the future' (*The Irish Times*, 9 December 2002). As such, it is intended to embrace a new social identity for both Dublin and Ireland.

Rather than provide another 'hero on horseback', the Council has offered us a piece of abstract art, which, while more difficult to appreciate, suggests a new sophistication in our relationship to the urban landscape. Vivenne Roche, a sculptor and member of the selection jury, describes the Spire as a 'signature' of Dublin for the rest of the world and, because of its sheer simplicity and lack of historical connotations, as 'an ideal emblem for the current times' (*The Irish Times*, 2 January 2001). Furthermore, the monument, which is purely secular but at the same time spectacular enough to invoke the transcendent, eclipses the church spires in the cityscape. In this sense, the Spire represents

[9] B. Arnold, *The Spire and Other Essays on Contemporary Culture*, Dublin: Liffey Press, 2003; T. P. Coogan, *Ireland in the Twentieth Century*, London: Hutchinson, 2004.

the transformation of social identity in a post-religious, post-rural and post-national Ireland. It re-positions us as urban and would-be-urbane Europeans, who have outgrown the old politics and ideologies and who seek to anchor ourselves in a shiny new future.

The Spire's significance goes beyond its imposing presence as a piece of public art on O'Connell Street or as a vehicle for economic regeneration. The citizens of Dublin have a mental map of the city configured around its key northside and southside co-ordinates. The postal code system – even numbers for the southside, odd numbers for the northside (with the exception of the President's residence and its environs) – allows for automatic categorisation. Property prices on the northside lag behind those on the southside even in the more salubrious neighbourhoods. The symbolic relations between the city's northside and southside are somewhat uneasy. Dublin humour is replete with pejorative jokes about northsiders. The *Phoenix* magazine playfully parodies our northside Taoiseach's diary, which makes generous use of Dublin street idioms. There is a world of difference between the 'cheap and cheerful' ambiance of Moore Street and Henry Street on the northern side of the river and the more 'pricey' feel to Grafton Street and its environs on the southern side.

Part of Dublin City Council's overall city strategy is to challenge the north/south division by creating an alternative east/west axis along the northern quays, with the National Museum at Collins Barracks at the western end and O'Connell Street at the eastern end. In this context, the Spire forms the centre point of a strategy to reverse the stereotyping of place in the city, and to encourage Dubliners to think about the spatial ordering of the city in a different way.

Conclusion

Art is frequently seen as somewhat detached from the everyday interests and concerns of the citizenry. In pursuing a controversial public art project as the centrepiece of the regeneration plan for O'Connell Street, Dublin City Council challenged this viewpoint. The municipality did so in the face of considerable public criticism particularly about the 'wastefulness' of spending public money on art rather than on hospitals and homeless shelters. Significantly, the Council was supported by influential lobbies from within the arts and business communities, as well as by local representatives on the IAP monitoring committee. A partnership of interests succeeded in bringing the Spire into being, not only as an aesthetic re-visioning of O'Connell Street but also as part of a wider strategy of civic boosterism for the north inner city.

The 'Spire of Dublin' is undoubtedly part of a commodity culture and it is already being deployed as a mechanism to get more consumers into O'Connell Street and its environs. But perhaps it also has the potential to be part of an anti-commodity culture. It challenges our aesthetic sensibility, and our received notions of how a monument should look and what it should represent. As public art it arrests our vision in a dramatic way both from a distance and close up. It reinforces the idea that the urban is now an embedded part of Irish social identity, and that we can aspire to the taste and sensibilities of our European counterparts.

CHAPTER 13

Brandcentral

İ. EMRE IŞIK

Brandcentral, the first discount designer outlet in the Republic of Ireland, opened on 7 November 2001. While most shopping malls are located in the immediate environs of the main cities in Ireland, this one is located in a small town in the midlands called Rathdowney. For many, the outlet's pre-opening billboard, newspaper and electronic media advertising campaigns were the first time they had heard of this small town. Even though Rathdowney is one of a number of small towns geographically located in the 'middle', it is not located anywhere within the speed-driven consumerist landscape of Ireland. Furthermore, Rathdowney found itself at the centre of a small controversy generated by the publication of an article[1] on the locality and its new outlet. This chapter will look at how Rathdowney – in the slow lane of the Celtic Tiger landscape, but with a new designer shopping outlet – is, and would like to be, perceived.

Dramatic changes in the Irish economy and Ireland's adaptation to global transformations have deeply affected the social life of towns and cities. The Irish economy is a prime example of reflexive accumulation, where the

1 R. Boland, 'If you build it, they will come', *The Irish Times Magazine*, 5 January 2002.

country's fate is no longer dictated by its geographical peripherality. It is the speed of information and its transmission that now determines peripherality. And social spaces do not operate at the same speed: 'some forces break or diminish speed, while others accelerate it'.[2] In this context, 'stasis is stigma' and, in a society where speed is the essence of all activities, exclusion is the fate of all those who are left behind.[3] The out-of-town shopping mall has been conceptualised as 'a particular kind of cathedral of consumption' proliferating as a feature of the process of ex-urbanisation.[4] Most of these malls are accessible by motorway and thus are designed to attract the driver-consumer and his or her family. They occupy premium space on the high-speed lane of modernity.

Henri Lefebvre and Michel de Certeau's conceptualisations of social space may be useful in analysing how places like Rathdowney are perceived, particularly in the context of changing social relations. According to Lefebvre, '(social) space is a (social) product' and physical space is disappearing.[5] Every mode of production produces its own space and within this production there are three distinctive and complementary levels. The first, spatial practices, highlights the issue of experience. The second is the representation of space, which is related to the conceptualisation of spatial practices by either ordinary people or experts. The third dimension is the space of representation, which is concerned with how space is invented and imagined. This third dimension has a transforming effect on the first two.

2 D. Kellner, 'Virilio, War and Technology: Some Critical Reflections', *Theory, Culture and Society*, vol. 16, no. 5-6, 1999, pp. 103-125, p. 103-4.

3 M. Cronin, 'Speed Limits: Ireland, Globalisation and the War against Time', in P. Kirby et al. (eds.), *Reinventing Ireland*, London: Pluto Press, 2002.

4 M. P. Corcoran, 'Mall City', in E. Slater and M. Peillon (eds.), *Memories of the Present: A Sociological Chronicle of Ireland 1997–1998*, Dublin: Institute of Public Administration, 2000, p. 92.

5 H. Lefebvre, *The Production of Space*, Oxford: Blackwell, 1992, p. 26.

Brandcentral entrance

For Lefebvre, social space, as an outcome of past actions, is what permits fresh actions and it becomes both the field of, and a basis for, action. The spatial practice of Rathdowney is to a large extent shaped by its relation to speed. But the representation of this space remains a contested matter. As a space of representation, Rathdowney aspires to join the high-speed lane of contemporary, consumerist Ireland.

De Certeau sees social space as open to social action and change. Everyday life consists of spatial practices and 'every story is a spatial story – a spatial practice'.[6] Here, place is considered as 'order' indicating a stability, and space, on the other hand, is conceived as the sum of mobile elements. Rathdowney's encounter with global transforming processes produces one such 'spatial story', where new spatial relations impact on place.

Rathdowney represented

Rathdowney may be said to be representative of many small towns dotted around Ireland. It has a population of approximately 1,300, with a catchment population of 6,000 (*Leinster Express*, 26 January 2002). The town itself consists of a main street with one other street branching off it, a town square, two local churches, two primary schools and a secondary school. The town is also served by the two main Irish banks and has a credit union. Meadow Meats, Arcon Mines and, more recently, Brandcentral are the three largest employers in the town. The smaller family-run grocery shops have been replaced by one large supermarket and several of the old variety sweetshops have long since closed down. Many of the locals travel further afield to Portlaoise, Thurles or Kilkenny to shop at discount stores like Aldi or Lidl. Architecturally, the town possesses no distinguishing features. It is a classical Irish town comprising two-storey and terraced housing interspersed with public houses.

Rathdowney considers itself open to transformations of social space. This is highlighted in an article from a local review, which argues that Rathdowney is no exception when one looks at the changing face of Irish towns (*Rathdowney Review*, 1985). The article takes us on a trip around the town:

---

6 M. de Certeau, *The Practice of Everyday Life*, London: University of California Press, 1988, p. 115.

The Square itself has changed little since the middle of the 1800s, the lime trees having been there for centuries, though some were felled and replaced only about 50 years ago. ...

Moving around the Square, it is so long since the Royal Bank and the Munster & Leinster Bank existed side by side until the merger in the early 70s. The two small homes in between were soon swallowed up by the new AIB while the Royal became P. P. Ryan's offices.

Tim Barry's was only recently vacated by Quigley-McGovern, but before that was owned by Dan Delaney (great-uncle of Pat Delaney, the Ossory). O'Malley's, always a lively spot, was no different under its former owners, Lalors, and for many years the corner was known as Lalor's corner. ...

Meadow Meats was Golden Vale and Lyons' and as everyone knows, Perry's Brewery kept the town of Rathdowney going for 140 years and the place has never been the same since!

This tour around the Square connects the present with the past of the town. Written by a local, it goes into details of shops, nature, streetscapes and people who are and were a part of change. It reflects on the everyday meanings and roles of both people and immobile elements, past and present, of the town space.

The biggest change that has come to Rathdowney, however, has been the arrival of Brandcentral. An article in *The Irish Times Magazine*, profiling Rathdowney and its new designer outlet, also begins with a small tour around the town.[7] This tour, however, was rather different in tone from the one authored by a local. The chip-shop called the Golden Cod, Boland writes, 'is not the only local establishment that has an aura of yellow shiny stuff about it' because five-minutes walk away is Brandcentral, which,

7 R. Boland, 'If you build it, they will come', *The Irish Times Magazine*, 5 January 2002.

'with a 420-million-euro price tag', 'could well be the golden goose'. The tour continues:

> At Campion's general store, where there is a stock of classic out-of-print John Hinde postcards of a donkey, they still do not sell top-up cards for mobile phones ... the window of Fortune's Fashions (closed for lunch) has a poster advertising a sponsored head-shave by staff of the local Modern Iron Works.
>
> The once-grand fountain on the main street (commemorating the death in 1918 of the wife of Alfred William Perry, the family which owned the long-since closed local brewery) no longer works and is full of rubbish.

Furthermore, Boland, in the course of researching this article, experiences intermittent loss of coverage on her mobile phone. She tells us 'there are very few places now in Ireland outside the mountains where coverage is particularly like this'. She feels disoriented, as if she were far west, instead of deep inland.

These disparaging comments elicited a strong reaction from locals, who found the article both factually and substantively incorrect. The price tag of €420 million was considerably inflated and should have read €42 million. The representation of Rathdowney as a dirty, archaic old village, backward and old-fashioned, was challenged in a discussion on the Marion Finucane show on RTÉ Radio 1 and in letters published in the national and local press. Local participants in these discussions felt that, contrary to the image created in the offending article, Rathdowney was a thriving small town with considerable social and economic vitality.

In terms of representation of space, these two differing interpretations of Rathdowney are examples of how locals and 'others' see social space from their own points of view. They highlight how local people's claim to normality and being part of the mainstream may clash with the view of the outsider. The reaction of the local people is a reaction to a possible place stereotype. 'A place stereotype', according to Sibley, 'might be a romantic representation of a landscape to which a social group are seen to belong or not, depending on the consistency or incongruity of the group and place stereotypes'; and 'a group can be in the "wrong" place if the stereotype locates it elsewhere'.[8]

In this context, it may be argued that Rathdowney's reaction to the aspersions cast in the article shows where Rathdowney wants itself to be located. *The Irish Times Magazine* profile located Rathdowney in the 'slower lane', whereas the locals have come to see themselves shifting up a gear into the 'fast lane' of Irish society. This is clearly expressed in the comment of a local that: 'property prices are up, there is a new confidence in the town and a sense of pride every time we hear Rathdowney on TV and see it on billboards around the country' (*Leinster Express*, 19 January 2002). Another local expresses her disappointment in relation to the article by saying that 'if you close your eyes and add another paragraph onto the article you can imagine her saying that children are going to school in their bare feet with sods of turf on their backs for the open fire in the school' (*Leinster Express*, 26 January 2002).

How to get to Brandcentral

Brandcentral is built on the foundations of an old textile factory and is a single-storey structure comprising individual shops and a large café/restaurant. With over 600 spaces, the car park offers ample parking for customers. It bears little resemblance to the malls and shopping centres with which we have become familiar, both in Ireland and abroad. Brandcentral in Rathdowney has a more pared-down, functional appearance. Its frontage, which consists of a wooden veranda, reminds one of the stage for a Hollywood

[8] D. Sibley, *Geographies of Exclusion*, London: Routledge, 1995, p. 100.

Getting to Brandcentral

western rather than a futuristic cathedral of consumption. In initial discussions, local concerns about any possible negative impact on grocery/retail business were allayed on learning that the development was not a shopping centre as such and would contain no grocery or newsagent units.

The Retail Operations Director of Brandcentral gives its distance from Dublin and its well-serviced central location on the road network (in the middle of two arterial routes between Dublin and Cork and Dublin and Limerick) as the reasons why Rathdowney was chosen as the site for the outlet. It was accepted by the developers that, although the road infrastructure was insufficient, the need to be in a central location was the primary consideration. This optimising of location is of course predicated on using a private car to get there. Even though it is possible to get close to Rathdowney by bus (to Borris-in-Ossory on the Limerick road and Cullohill on the Cork road) and by train (to Ballybrophy) it still requires a taxi trip or a well-researched effort by visitors to ascertain the times of local, privately run buses to actually reach Rathdowney itself. The need to provide directions to the location of the outlet proved a challenge for the advertising campaigns. Directions were given as Rathdowney, near Portlaoise. Later, these were changed and given as Rathdowney, near Abbeyleix. This confusion was eased somewhat with signposts erected on all of the main routes to the town.

The Retail Operations Director identifies the target customers (mainly women) as those within a fifty-mile radius of the town, and notes that 'for somebody travelling down from Dublin, the journey takes two hours, there are only sixteen stores and so their expectations would be shattered'.[9] It is this sense of disappointment that suffuses *The Irish Times Magazine* article: 'This was my first time visiting a designer outlet anywhere, and I was expecting, well, designer shops. But this is Ireland and we never seem to get things quite right, Brandcentral as it is, is best described as a sort of Lucky Bag'.

Conclusion

Neither Brandcentral nor Rathdowney are likely to leave a promising image in the minds of the readers of the article in *The Irish Times Magazine*. Lack of services, in this case mainly public transport, and the image presented of those who live in the 'middle', highlight the distance between the core and the peripheries. 'Speed' in the new Ireland is transforming socio-spatial relations by creating new rhythms and types of interactions that are unequal and fragmented in their nature. Acceleration to high speed in every part of the new consumerist landscape does not seem possible. Thus, it is interesting that *The Irish Times Magazine* journalist writes of being disoriented by the mobile coverage disruption, which made her feel as if she was 'far west', a place almost invariably associated with slowing down, relaxation and generally getting away from speed.

9 www.iavi.ie/stumag/2002_1/4.asp

Not only are some groups left behind in the speed race, but also places are produced as new geographical peripheries and are consigned to the slow lane of the race track. Some of these slow lanes may be advantaged because of their location or may occupy an important place in the collective memory of the public because of their history or nature, but others do not. In this respect, midland towns like Rathdowney find themselves on the margins, and perhaps more so than parts of Ireland that we historically have thought of as marginal or peripheral. In many ways, smaller midland towns are merely places passed on the way to other places, seen as signposts on the roadside. They are neither tourist attractions nor cultural/economic centres. Rathdowney imagines itself, and wishes to be imagined, as part of contemporary high-speed Irish society. Its town space changed with the coming of Brandcentral and it can be said that such new development reshapes spatial relations both in the town itself and in its relation to a wider national space. Seeing and hearing the name of the town in the media is a source of pride and confidence for the locals. After all, it is primarily their lived space, prior to it being perceived by others.

CHAPTER 14

The Making of the Dublin Conurbation

MICHEL PEILLON

With the publication of the *National Spatial Strategy for Ireland 2002-2020*, urban development has come to the fore as a policy issue. It is proposed that the existing urban space will be used more systematically and a higher density encouraged: this will happen through the consolidation of existing settlements, the redevelopment of central urban areas and the re-allocation of under-utilised land and buildings. The addition of an anticipated half a million dwellings over the period 2002 to 2020 will involve the growth and development of areas surroundings cities and towns, particularly Dublin.

The document does not refer to suburbs as such. It states that the creation of completely new cities or towns is not required and that the strategy also aims to minimise 'urban sprawl'. Urban sprawl is a codeword for the kind of suburban and peri-urban development that has taken place around the main cities in Ireland in the recent past. Peripheral suburban development (or the emergence of commuter towns) is not considered to be desirable or even sustainable:

> Housing pressures in the Greater Dublin Area and the improvements in the road and rail network radiating from

> Dublin, have encouraged extensive commuter based development at some considerable distance from the Greater Dublin Area. As a by-product of unbalanced spatial development, this long distance commuter based development is generally unsustainable. Building up critical mass in other regions, to complement Dublin, is central to countering this trend.[1]

The National Spatial Strategy (NSS) argues that the midlands should not become a dormitory for Dublin-based workers and that surrounding counties should not be subsumed into the urban sprawl of a greater Dublin. The balance in urban development will come from the designation of strategically placed urban centres, labelled hubs and gateways.

Dispersed city

The NSS makes reference to the tendency of Dublin to become a dispersed city, and it talks about hi-tech industries locating at the city's edge:

> There is strong evidence that Dublin is becoming a 'Dispersed City' demonstrated by the fact that the hi-tech industries located around the city's edges are drawing their workforces from places up to and beyond 80 kilometres away, but within an hour's drive of people's workplaces. New hotels, major industrial parks, technology campuses, out-of-town shopping centres, suburban business and office parks, improved roads, relatively low road fuel prices, higher car ownership and availability and use of certain commuter train services have created an increasingly dispersed form of growth in the [Greater Dublin Area] and beyond.[2]

1 Department of the Environment and Local Government, *National Spatial Strategy for Ireland 2002-2020: People, Places and Potential*, Dublin: Government Publications, 2002, p. 44.

2 ibid., p. 22.

This kind of vocabulary – dispersion, edge – assumes a classical model of the metropolis, with its downtown centre, and then suburban and peripheral areas that depend on the centre for the provision of a wide range of services. This is, etymologically, what is meant by sub-urb: not fully urban because it is located at a distance from the core. Dispersal occurs when services and urban development move away from the urban centre on which they depend. The NSS is an attempt to contain this dispersal in metropolitan growth by developing urban centres that counterbalance the impact of the metropolis or other large cities. But the 'dispersion' of Dublin may actually point to a very different kind of urban development: not as a metropolis gone mad, not as a regional balancing of urban centres, but as what has been referred to as a poly-nucleated conurbation.[3]

Ex-centred urban design

[3] M. Gottdiener, *The Social Production of Urban Space*, Austin: University of Texas Press, 1994.

Beyond suburbia

Since the mid-1990s, suburban development has taken place in locations that can only be characterised as rural. This kind of peripheral suburban development is well illustrated by Ratoath in County Meath, which was the focus of a recent survey.[4] A very small place until the mid-1980s, Ratoath has since increased its population tenfold. It provides a good example of a peripheral development, not very far from central Dublin, but nonetheless 'beyond suburbia', as one advertisement for new housing in Ratoath put it.

Respondents in the survey were asked a question about where they went to avail of a range of services: shopping, banking, recreation, socialising etc. Their replies are summarised in Table 1. Availing of a wide range of services is quite clearly patterned in a spatial way. Some services are availed of locally: post office, church, pub, primary school, doctor. Quite unexpectedly, two further activities also take place predominantly in Ratoath: sporting activities and eating out. The neighbouring towns of Ashbourne and Dunshaughlin are relied upon for shopping and banking. These services were not available in Ratoath at the time of the survey; a small supermarket has opened since. But a substantial number of Ratoath residents also go to these towns for medical services and, to a lesser extent, for school and sporting activities. The commercial centre at Blanchardstown represents a powerful attraction for shopping and going to the cinema, with some use of the banks there. Dublin, which never seems central to the life of Ratoath residents, rates high only for music venues and banking (probably close to work for some). One would expect Dublin to play a more significant role in relation to recreation (such as cinema going) or socialising (such as

[4] This information was obtained as part of the New Urban Living Study, conducted by Mary P. Corcoran, Jane Gray and Michel Peillon. The first phase of the study involved a survey of Ratoath residents.

Table 1. Locations where Ratoath residents avail of services (%), 2002

Activity	*Within Ratoath*	*Neighbouring towns*	*Blanchards-town*	*Dublin*	*Others**
Post office	88	–	1	1	10
Church	68	1	–	–	30
Pub	73	1	–	4.5	21.5
Sporting activities	33	6	6	7.5	47.5
Restaurant	57	1.5	–	9.5	32
Doctor	69	16	–	6.5	8.5
School	42	4	–	4	50
Shopping (supermarket)	3	27	41	3	26
Bank	–	39	12	24	25
Cinema	–	–	68	6	26
Music (concerts etc.)	4	–	1	41	54

* Some respondents did not avail of particular services.

pubs and restaurants), but the contribution of Dublin in this respect remains quite limited.

An important aspect is missing in the figures in Table 1: work. A question was asked about how long it took people to travel to work. It would normally take, at peak times, 45 minutes to an hour to travel to, or from, Dublin. Roughly 44 per cent of respondents for whom the question was relevant faced a journey of between half an hour and one hour. Among these 44 per cent, it remains difficult to estimate the proportion of those who actually work in central Dublin. The high number of Ratoath respondents employed in the information technology sector would suggest that a significant proportion travel to places on the periphery of Dublin (such as Swords or Leixlip). One can tentatively estimate that one-third of working respondents travel to Dublin for work.

A night out at the edge

A conurbation in the making

If we leave out of our consideration the location of work for Ratoath residents, the emergence of Ratoath as a residential location is not necessarily best understood in terms of suburbanisation, which assumes a dependence on an urban centre such as Dublin. It makes sense in terms of another form of urban development that Dublin may be experiencing, that of a diffuse conurbation: 'these poly-nucleated regions are no longer organized by the sociospatial activities of the historic city center. Words, such as "urban" and "rural", which were once used to categorize places have now lost their analytical value'.[5]

[5] M. Gottdiener, *The Social Production of Urban Space*, Austin: University of Texas Press, 1994, p. 8.

This has a resonance for a place like Ratoath, which is defined by residents as country-like, or having a country feel, while of course becoming less and less rural. The low reliance of Ratoath residents on Dublin and the selective use, along very functional lines, of proximate centres – either neighbouring towns or large peripheral commercial centres (and probably working in similar peripheral industrial estates) – point to the organisation of the daily life of Ratoath residents around several 'centres', which are treated as preferable alternatives to Dublin. The life of Ratoath residents, although fully part of an urban setting, is certainly 'poly-centred'. Such residents already belong to a conurbation that does not conform, at least for them, to a metropolis. If the mode of inclusion of Ratoath residents in the Dublin urban texture is typical of things to come, then it could be realistically contended that Dublin is moving away from the metropolitan model and transforming itself into a conurbation.

The NSS appears anxious to avoid such a development, and the proposed midlands gateway linking Athlone, Mullingar and Tullamore is thought to be located far enough from Dublin to counterbalance it – rather than being absorbed into one large, poly-centred, eastern conurbation. But this strategy remains risky, as an urban centre such as Mullingar is already becoming part of the commuter belt. The NSS could easily experience a slippage and promote, as an unintended consequence, the development of a poly-nucleated conurbation on the east coast that would draw on urban centres in the midlands.

An urban fabric linking several towns constitutes one version of multi-centred urban development. A multiplication of small centres offers a more realistic scenario for Dublin. These emergent centres have been referred to, in another context, as 'edge cities'.[6] Edge cities are not located in town centres, and they are no longer suburbs. They

[6] J. Garreau, *Edge City. Life on the New Frontier*, New York: Anchor Books Doubleday, 1992.

It's all there

appear in often unexpected locations, sometimes simply at strategic traffic junctions. As industrial campuses, they create jobs and attract headquarters of corporations. Their extensive shopping malls function as new marketplaces. The presence of cinemas, restaurants and bars, as well as spacious hotels, transform them into entertainment places. With the provision of various administrative services, they may even become civic centres in their own right. People may stroll in the parks and congregate in the plazas that are sometimes included in their design. A conurbation is dotted with such ex-centred urban crystallisations. The label of edge city could easily mislead: suggesting as it does a model of centre and periphery, which it is meant to overcome. In fact, when these urban cores have multiplied, the edge of the city has really disappeared.

Greater Dublin has grown according to a model of suburbanisation in which shopping malls opened at peripheral locations and industrial firms settled in remote but usually convenient locations. The functions of such spaces were specialised. But their character changed slowly: industrial estates became marketplaces for a range of retail trades. Shopping centres turned into places of entertainment, with cinemas and restaurants. Hotels and lounges moved close by or located within. Many civic and cultural agencies (library, galleries, theatres) set up store there. New (and possibly ex-centred) town centres have been designed and built around the accumulation of such urban functions.

Dublin possesses a very low, traditional skyline, dominated by church spires. For many years, only Liberty Hall and the Central Bank, which have long been viewed with distaste and disapproval, competed with them. Recently, a few high-rise buildings have been allowed on both sides of the Docks. The Spire (see Chapter 12) is effective only because of the low profile of its surroundings. But many of the new tall buildings are not rising at the centre of Dublin. They are being erected in large business campuses and in new multi-functional spaces. If a city is characterised by its height, the urban feel has moved away from the centre of Dublin.

Post-industrial metropolis

Gottdiener explicitly links the emergence of a poly-centred conurbation with the development of a post-industrial capitalism: 'According to my perspective, the multicentered metropolitan region is the phenomenal socio-spatial form of late capitalism'.[7] Garreau too accounts for the emergence of edge cities in terms of the information society. But the contrary argument has also been put forward.

Sassen argues that the post-industrial economy 'requires the massive concentration of human and telecommunication resources we find in major cities'.[8] Global cities, that is cities which enjoy a strategic position within the global economy, concentrate administrative functions and offer specialised producer services: financial, legal, design,

7 M. Gottdiener, *The Social Production of Urban Space*, Austin: University of Texas Press, 1994, p. x.

8 S. Sassen, 'Cities in the Global Economy', in G. Browning, A. Halcli and F. Webster (eds.), *Understanding Contemporary Society. Theories of the Present*, London: Sage, 1999, p. 269.

communication etc. Sassen contends that such services must be located within the city, and that they must converge at its centre. This concentration within the city centre occurs for two main reasons. It has to do, first of all, with the need for a very dense infrastructure that, even in the age of global information flows, is neither flexible nor mobile. The performance of firms in the post-industrial economy is also helped by the geographical concentration of the relevant labour force. The latter facilitates a close interaction between those involved in specialised fields. This proximity encourages a sociability, which promotes the exchange of ideas and generates useful networks.

This approach seems to have motivated major projects in the recent development of Dublin. The International Financial Services Centre, at the very heart of Dublin, now employs around 10,000 people, most of them in skilled occupations. It operates as a kind of offshore financial centre. Also in the city centre, Temple Bar has been developed as Dublin's cultural centre and as a touristic attraction. In the process, it has become the main entertainment area of Dublin, with many bars, restaurants and discos. In 2000, the development of two digital hubs was announced in a sustained effort to promote the multimedia industry: one in the Liberties in central Dublin and the other at Citywest in the suburbs of Dublin. Such a choice demonstrates the flexibility of this kind of industry. It could easily be located in the Liberties, a highly symbolic part of the old Dublin close to the city centre and its cultural/entertainment district. But it could also be moved away from this core.

The labour force in many of these post-industrial sectors of activity is both young and highly educated. Unwilling to reside in the suburbs and anxious to satisfy their cultural and social needs, they choose to live at the centre. Highly mobile, they seek places of employment which offer a lifestyle that suits them. They have given an impetus to the regeneration of many areas close to the city centre. They also have been associated with apartment living in Dublin

Headquarters in the business campus

and with what has been referred to as its gentrification. The post-industrial, global economy has, after all, strengthened the metropolis.

Conclusion

The three scenarios of urban development that have been identified in this chapter are all observed in the context of Dublin. The apparent suburbanisation of Dublin is turning into something quite different. It is absorbing towns that functioned as urban centres in their own right. The urban fabric that is slowly woven in and around Dublin includes many such centres. Meanwhile Dublin's historic core may be losing some of its functions. Many Ratoath residents live their lives in a way that does not involve Dublin centre, relying instead on a range of proximate centres. This pattern of development involves the emergence of new centres that increasingly fulfil the functions of the city: they provide employment, function as new marketplaces and offer a range of entertainment facilities. Administrative and cultural services increasingly gravitate around these 'edge cities'. If employment, trade and entertainment are moving away from central Dublin, the latter simply ceases to be the centre of Dublin. Yet, for some categories of residents, the metropolitan core of Dublin has been strengthened in many ways.

These three patterns of urban development have each been linked with the late-capitalist or post-industrial economy. It would appear that post-industrial growth is compatible with various urban forms, at least in the Dublin context. The formation of a 'poly-centred conurbation', the emergence of edge cities and the strengthening of the metropolitan core are occurring simultaneously. 'As usual, it's all ad hoc: we're making this up as we go along'.[9] Although it clearly retains relevance for Dublin, this comment does not bemoan the lack of anticipation and planning in public decision-making in Ireland, but relates to the American experience of urban development.

[9] J. Garreau, *Edge City. Life on the New Frontier*, New York: Anchor Books Doubleday, 1992, p. xx.

PART 4

TENSIONS AND CONTRAVENTIONS

Bóthar from focail.com by Seán Hillen and Ruán Magan, 2003

Details from *NOW:HERE* by Garrett Phelan, 2003, permanent marker on wall, Dublin City Council flat

Journey to the Centre of the Blanchardstown Roundabout by Alan Phelan, 2003, duratran photograph with solar powered turning mechanism, PVC, self-adhesive vinyl, paint, video monitor, VHS video player
Installation size: 225 high x 125 wide cms
Video duration: 3 minutes

Falling 1 by Cris Neuman, 2003, cardboard on panel, 15" x 10" x 2"

CHAPTER 15

The Land of Conditional Welcomes

GERARD W. BOUCHER

Central Statistics Office figures show that it was only in 1996 that Ireland officially became a country of net immigration, much later than most other EU member states.

One might have expected that Irish popular attitudes towards, and treatment of, immigrants would be conditioned by the history, stories and personal experiences of Irish emigration: in host societies, Irish economic immigrants were not always welcomed or treated well historically. But neither the memory nor the legacy of Irish emigration seems to inform attitudes towards contemporary immigrants in Ireland.

This lack of social learning by Irish people has been accompanied by a lack of policy learning by the Irish state. Again, one might have expected that the state's migration policy would be based on 'best practices' determined by the wide variety of experiences of immigration in other European countries. Generally this has not been the case. The state has in fact adopted a 'Fortress Europe' approach to asylum seekers, who have been 'criminalised' and policed in line with the EU Treaty of Amsterdam, and dispersed and directly provisioned following UK policy.

As Mac Éinrí notes, the majority of migrants who arrive to work in the Irish labour market are subjected to a short-term 'market-driven approach'.[1] This policy shows little learning from the experiences of countries like Germany, which relied on a *gastarbeiter* or guestworker policy and wrongly assumed that the 'guests' would go home after a short time and not become permanent residents and raise families in the host country.

In the Irish case, the major policy gap has been a lack of co-ordination between the asylum, refugee, labour market and EU and EEA immigration and the integration of non-Irish migrants into Irish society. This is surprising given that, in interviews[2] with twenty-two representatives drawn mostly from social partnership organisations and state bodies, there was a broad consensus that the Irish state needed a comprehensive and co-ordinated immigration policy.

Arguably, Ireland's lack of a comprehensive and co-ordinated immigration policy has resulted in contradictions between the various policy areas of immigration and integration, between and within the government departments responsible for these policies, and in the daily experiences of immigrants in Irish society. As such, Ireland has become a land of conditional welcomes. Whether and to what extent newcomers are made to feel welcome is predicated on a number of factors including the immigrant's categorisation, access to rights, level of state intervention in the migrant's life and day-to-day experiences in Irish society.

---

1 P. Mac Éinrí, 'Towards a Strategic Immigration Policy: Some Key Elements', Cork: Irish Centre for Migration Studies, pp. 3-4, http://migration.ucc.ie/immigration.htm

2 The interviews were conducted in 2002 as part of Project 'Flexcom' – Flexibility and Competitiveness: Labour Market Flexibility, Innovation and Organisational Performance (funded by the European Commission within the IHP Programme, contract no. HPSE-CT-2001-0093).

This chapter explores some of these issues. It begins with a portrait of immigration in Ireland in 2002, which leads to a discussion, first, of the different forms that conditional welcomes take at institutional and societal levels, and, second, on the state's fragmented and contradictory immigration policy. Finally, it examines some of the institutional, political and socio-cultural reasons that may help to explain the continued lack of a comprehensive and co-ordinated Irish immigration policy.

Profile of immigration in 2002

The Irish Census of 2002 reveals that, of the people normally resident in the Republic of Ireland, 89 per cent were born in the Republic, 7 per cent in the UK, 1 per cent in other EU states, and 3 per cent outside the EU. However, not everyone born outside the state is necessarily non-Irish. According to the 2002 Census, the proportion of non-Irish people resident in Ireland is just over 6 per cent and most of these are from the UK or other EU states. The proportion of Irish residents from non-EU European states, Africa, Asia, America and Australia/New Zealand therefore remains very low (around 2 per cent).

Yet, much of the popular, official and academic debate about Ireland's historical transformation to a country of immigration focuses on the reception of the relatively small percentage of non-white and Eastern European asylum seekers and refugees, and on the topics of racism and anti-racism.

The immigration figures for 2002 suggest that this focus is not comprehensive enough. Of the roughly forty-seven thousand people who migrated to Ireland in that year, approximately one-quarter arrived as asylum seekers, almost one-half on work permits and another five per cent or so on work visas and authorisations. Thus, over fifty per cent of all official migrants to Ireland in 2002 arrived as official labour market immigrants on permits and visas.

If Ireland follows the pattern of earlier countries of immigration, a significant proportion of these immigrants will become permanent Irish residents and citizens, and will bring over their families or find partners and have children in Ireland. The lack of a comprehensive and co-ordinated immigration policy has contributed to a lack of public debate about the long-term integration of these immigrants into Irish society.

One welcome will do

Cead míle fáilte, one hundred thousand welcomes, is an Irish language expression that is often used on official occasions to greet representatives of foreign governments and organisations arriving in Ireland. *Fáilte* is also part of the tourist board's Irish language name, representing the official welcoming image of Ireland marketed to potential tourists abroad. However, it is not an expression that one hears or sees used officially to welcome immigrants entering Ireland.

Instead, immigrants to Ireland are immediately channelled into official categories such as asylum seeker, programme refugee, and work-permit, visa or authorisation holder, each subject to different rights and policing arrangements. These categories, rights and arrangements are derived from UN conventions, EU law and agreements, as well as Irish law and institutional practices. The effect of this de facto stratification is that immigrants to Ireland are subjected to conditional welcomes, depending on their official immigrant status.

Irish conditional welcomes continue for immigrants living in Ireland. The lives of asylum seekers are strictly controlled through a policy of dispersion and direct provision; the jobs of work-permit holders are tied to their employers; and, while work-visa holders are allowed to change employers within their sector, they do not have the right to social welfare, free medical care or education. In practice, these rules are not always enforced and it is common enough, for example, for asylum seekers to move from their officially assigned domicile to their emerging ethnic communities in cities or for work-permit holders to change employers.

The Irish state's rather rigid treatment of immigrants *entering* the country is to some extent offset by its often lax treatment of those same immigrants *living* in the country. The extent of the state's intervention in the immigrant's life varies according to official categories. Asylum seekers are by far the most controlled and policed group of immigrants, while those on student and work visas are rarely subject to intervention. The Irish state does not overly concern itself with the day-to-day integration of legal immigrants in Irish society.

With the state hardly involved in the integration process, the conditionality of Irish welcomes is extended into the daily life of newcomers. Integration is, by and large, left to the individual, family, ethnic community, friends, state agency and labour market. Therefore, the immigrant's daily experience may be fragmented and contradictory. For example, a typical immigrant's day-to-day experience may include: friendliness by some Irish people and direct discrimination by others; pressure to assimilate to Irish practices and counter-pressure to remain separate within one's ethnic community; the creation of new practices between the immigrant and Irish friends; and civil treatment as well as institutional discrimination by representatives of the Irish state.

A fragmented and contradictory immigration policy

This fragmented and often contradictory treatment of immigrants is sometimes reflected in a single government department. Thus, the Department of Justice, Equality and Law Reform enforces the Irish version of 'Fortress Europe' within the UK and Ireland Common Travel Zone. The department has overall responsibility for immigration and citizenship law and control of immigration, including asylum seekers and refugees. It created the Reception and Integration Agency to oversee the dispersal and direct provision programme. The term 'integration' applies here only to asylum seekers and its use is contradictory: the agency transports asylum seekers upon arrival to hostels and other group residences, usually in less-populated areas, where they are expected to remain until the asylum application procedure is complete. Only in Orwell's doublespeak could 'integration' mean 'forced segregation'.

Yet, the department also incorporates the Equality Authority (which actively works to promote non-discrimination) and the National Consultative Committee on Racism and Interculturalism (which develops anti-racism and intercultural programmes and actions). The remits of these two state bodies seem to be at direct variance with some of the policies implemented by the department itself, particularly with respect to the current treatment of asylum seekers.

At the same time, the Department of Enterprise, Trade and Employment administers the work permits programme, under which the majority of immigrants arrived in 2002. To make things more complex, the Department of Foreign Affairs has played a leading role in the immigration of programme refugees; and it administers work visas and authorisations in its embassies and consulates, with the Department of Justice, Equality and Law Reform retaining overall responsibility. These employer-based immigration schemes appear to be run separately from the rest of Irish immigration policy. For example, the education, skills and work experience of asylum seekers in Ireland are not matched to jobs required by Irish employers who seek employees abroad to come to Ireland on permits, visas and authorisations.

The fragmented, contradictory nature of the Irish immigration system has not gone unnoticed, even within government. Thus, the Interdepartmental Working Group on the Integration of Refugees in Ireland stated in terms that could apply broadly to Irish immigration policy that:

> In the absence of a co-ordinated national policy on integration ... the measures taken by the state to facilitate integration have been fragmented and lacking in co-ordination ... there must be cohesion in delivery of services and the Government's commitment to integration must be clearly grounded in Government policy.[3]

Two of the main employers' bodies involved in social partnership have gone further, advocating a singly administered comprehensive immigration policy. For the Irish Business and Employers' Confederation, this administrative body should have 'one single administrative procedure, combining entry visas and work/study/permit applications and renewals'; while for the Chambers of Commerce of Ireland, a 'new executive agency' called 'the National Immigration Authority' should 'ensure the efficient implementation of all aspects of economic immigration policy'.[4]

As noted above, these official views are broadly confirmed by the twenty-two interviews with state and social partner representatives as part of Project 'Flexcom'. For example, a respondent from the National Economic and Social Council criticised the market-driven approach to immigration adopted by the state, arguing that 'there is a need for a clearer long-term policy on migration beyond the ad hoc policies based on market and supply demand factors'. Further, a representative of the Irish Congress of Trade Unions proclaimed that 'We need a coordinated integrated immigration policy ... Currently, we are getting mixed messages confusing asylum-seekers, refugees and migrant workers'.

---

3 Department of Justice, Equality and Law Reform, *Integration A Two Way Process*, Dublin: Government Publications, 1999, p. 20. The working group included representatives from eight government departments.

4 Irish Business and Employers' Confederation, *Social Policy in a Competitive Economy*, Dublin: IBEC 2002, p. 17; Chambers of Commerce of Ireland, *Labour Force 2001 Economic Immigration*, Dublin: CCI, 2001, p. 2.

Why is there no comprehensive and co-ordinated immigration policy?

There is broad agreement within the Irish state and social partnership organisations that a comprehensive and co-ordinated Irish immigration policy is needed. Yet, it does not exist. There are a number of institutional, political and socio-cultural factors that may help to explain this situation.

- *Institutional factors*

The first institutional reason concerns the time it takes for institutions to innovate in response to new policy demands. Ireland has been a country of immigration for less than ten years and the state has been fairly innovative in terms of policy changes. It has, for instance, created new bodies like the National Consultative Committee on Racism and Interculturalism and the Reception and Integration Agency; established programmes such as the work visa scheme; and passed new legislation dealing with immigration and citizenship including the Refugee Act, 1996, Immigration Act, 1999, Illegal Immigrants (Trafficking) Act, 2000, Irish National and Citizenship Act, 2001 and the Employment Permits Act, 2003. From this perspective, it is mostly a matter of time before the state develops a comprehensive and co-ordinated immigration policy.

The second reason undercuts the first by stressing the importance of institutional traditions and of conflicts between state agencies over resources, power and prestige. As Fanning[5] shows, the current division of labour over immigration policy between the three government departments has its roots in the development of Irish immigration policy from the 1930s through to the 1950s. Its main concern was the maintenance of strict control over which 'aliens' entered the country in order to ensure that foreigners did not take jobs from Irish citizens and to avoid immigrants of any category becoming a burden on the state.

5 B. Fanning, *Racism and Social Change in the Republic of Ireland*, Manchester: Manchester University Press, 2002.

While the former Department of Justice had primary responsibility for this policy area, both the precursors to the Department of Enterprise, Trade and Employment and the Department of Foreign Affairs had important subsidiary roles. To create a new state agency to co-ordinate immigration policy would upset the traditional balance of power between these departments, most likely in favour of the Department of Justice, Equality and Law Reform – the front runner to 'house' the new agency. It would also increase the costs of administering Irish immigration policy. Thus, the consensus about the need for a comprehensive and co-ordinated immigration policy does not extend to which department should run it or which departments would have to divert funds in order to pay for it.

- *Political factors*

This institutional inertia might be overcome with sufficient political pressure from the government or electorate. However, the neo-liberal coalition government of Fianna Fáil and the Progressive Democrats in power since 1997 promotes an agenda of intense policing of asylum seekers and undocumented immigrants, as well as a 'free market' perspective on labour immigration. It is unlikely that such a coalition would agree to create a new state agency for immigration, let alone exercise the political will necessary to overcome institutional resistance.

There is little evidence of electoral support for a comprehensive and co-ordinated immigration policy. Instead, there is much anecdotal evidence from canvassers in the 2002 national election that far too many Irish people believe that asylum seekers abuse the Irish state, that foreigners are taking Irish jobs and that Irish immigration policy is not strict enough. If these beliefs are widespread, it becomes difficult for the government to push for a more progressive immigration policy. At the same time, there is little evidence that government members are willing to challenge these popular beliefs in official speeches, media appearances, constituency clinics or on the doorstep of people's homes.

- *Socio-cultural factors*

Even if the political will existed to create a comprehensive and co-ordinated immigration policy, official economic nationalism and popular cultural self-denial might lead to additional problems of support and implementation.

In terms of the former, those interviewed as part of Project 'Flexcom' stress that the state narrowly focuses on immigration (outside of asylum-seeking) in terms of labour market supply and demand. No-one expected the Celtic Tiger boom to last as long as it did, to lead to labour and skill shortages or to attract large numbers of immigrants. It was expected that, when the boom ended, unemployment and emigration would increase again. Should this occur, it is believed that existing jobs should go to Irish people and immigrants should go 'home' unless their skills are needed. Thus, what appears to be simply a neo-liberal market approach to immigration is actually an expression of the economic nationalism that underlies the traditional policy on labour immigration.

With respect to cultural self-denial, it is not so long ago that Irish society was characterised as having a 'dependency syndrome'.[6] A dependency culture existed alongside a flourishing informal economy. Many Irish economic immigrants carried this cultural baggage with them, for example working illegally in the US or claiming the dole both in Ireland and the UK. While tribunals have focused attention on the corruption of the wealthy, there has been little public discussion of the everyday corruption that pervades Irish society. Instead, this repressed cultural knowledge appears to be projected onto asylum seekers and foreign others, scapegoats for the anger and moral outrage that the 'Irish' would not turn on themselves. They deflect onto immigrants the very qualities of 'sponging' and 'cheating' that they recognise in themselves, but which they prefer to deny. It is unlikely that a 'Know Racism' campaign[7]

6 J. Lee, *Ireland 1912-1985*, Cork: Cork University Press, 1989, p. 560.

7 Know Racism is a national anti-racism awareness programme, see www.knowracism.ie for further details.

can effectively breach this level of cultural self-denial or transform it into support for a comprehensive and co-ordinated immigration policy.

Conclusion

Since the mid-1990s, Ireland has become more of a cosmopolitan, multicultural and multiracial society than previously. The formation of intercultural Ireland is happening now. Even a severe economic downturn would not lead a large proportion of the new immigrants to 'go home'. They have endured the conditional welcomes and many have already made Ireland their new home.

Official policy needs to catch up to the social reality that Ireland is a country of immigration, which requires a comprehensive and co-ordinated policy to ensure the long-term integration of immigrants into Irish society. There is much support within the state and the expanded community of social partners for a progressive approach to immigration and a policy of integration that extends beyond the rhetoric of *cead míle fáilte.*

CHAPTER 16

Cows in Dublin, Public Spaces and Public Transport

JAMES WICKHAM

Statues of cows appeared on the streets of Dublin in 2003. The cows were of different colours and shapes. One had wings. Dublin, like many other European cities, was participating in an initiative to locate temporary statues in public spaces. After a few days, some of the cows were removed from public access into protective custody because they had been vandalised – the wings of the winged cow had even been cut off. Dublin's unique spirit had once again triumphed – in every other city the cows remained happily in public pastures.

Why did the cows get cut up? Nobody, to my knowledge, has suggested the obvious answer, which is that the cows were vandalised because Luas, Dublin's new tram system that was meant to start running in 2002, was not yet working. Perhaps that is not quite fair, but this chapter argues that there is a connection between such misuse of public space in Dublin and the city's lack of public transport.

The first part of the chapter links citizenship to public spaces and hence to public transport. The more empirical parts of the chapter use some data from an EU-funded research project to show how the failings of Dublin's public transport 'system' generates social exclusion and the loss of social cohesion.[1] The conclusion claims that using public transport is one way in which citizens can learn the rights and duties of urban citizenship – including the obligation not to cut up statues.

From public places to public transport

Those vandalised cows were in 'public places'. Roads are public places, but on a road you are expected to be in a car. By contrast, pavements, plazas and parks are for everyone – so that is where public art is placed. Furthermore, whereas roads fulfil one function, public places such as parks are open to different uses. Such places are public in that they are publicly controlled, they are the property of the public (the local authority or whatever) and they are for use by citizens.

The city is a physical space for citizenship. People who live in the same city, even if they do not live in the same neighbourhood, share common physical places and common physical spaces. The city is a space used by strangers who nonetheless have something in common. In the words of Richard Sennett: '"City" and "civility" have a common root etymologically. Civility is treating others as though they were strangers and forging a social bond upon that social distance'.[2] Civility, furthermore, connects with the duties of citizenship. Public transport is crucial in this regard: it literally ties the city together. Public transport increases the chances that all citizens can have access to the same spaces.

1 Project 'SceneSusTech – Scenarios for Sustainable Technology: Car-systems in the City and the Sociology of Embedded Technologies' (1998–2000). Funded by the European Commission within the Targeted Socio-Economic Research (TSER) Programme of the Fourth Framework Programme. Contract number: SOE1-CT97-1071. Full details of the project, including the full final report and more detailed individual reports, are available at the Employment Research Centre website: www.tcd.ie/erc/cars.

2 R. Sennett, *The Fall of Public Man*, Harmondsworth: Penguin Books, 2002 [1986], p. 264.

Being a citizen of a city involves the right to move around the city and to share this right with other citizens. This right to mobility is shared with visitors (and, in this sense, the city is far more welcoming than the nation state, which reserves many of its welfare facilities for national citizens).

Sociological discussion of citizenship has spent more time on the rights of citizenship than on its duties, yet legal theory shows that rights necessarily involve restraints on the rights of others.[3] My right to cheap transport constrains your right to spend your income. Furthermore, once people have rights, they are also opened up to duties. Thus the right to public space imposes on us the duty of appropriate public behaviour (civility) towards others in that space. The only way to avoid this duty is not to exercise the right – and to withdraw to private space.[4] Graffiti, littering and other loutish or threatening behaviour indicate that the perpetrator exercises his or her use of the facility at the cost of others. Such behaviour has, of course, a simple consequence: other citizens abandon the facility as soon as they can, for example by swapping public for private forms of transport. Public spaces become uncivil.

Dublin's mobility in perspective

The empirical part of this chapter derives from research on mobility in four European cities. Two cities – Athens and Dublin – were chosen as cities characterised by high levels of car usage and notorious traffic chaos. Two other cities – Bologna and Helsinki – had reputations for relatively good public transport and quite effective restraints on the private motor car. Part of the study involved 'zooming in' on three areas in each city, defined roughly as 'working-class

3 U. Pagano, 'Rights, Liberties and Institutional Complementarities', European Association for Evolutionary Political Economy (EAEPE) Conference, 2001.

4 R. Beauregard and A. Bounds, 'Urban citizenship', in E. Isin (ed.), *Democracy, Citizenship, and the Global City*, London: Routledge, 2000.

suburban', 'middle-class suburban' and 'new professional inner-city', indicated in Figure 1 as W, M and I respectively. Within each area we carried out ethnographic observation, a social survey and focus group interviews. This chapter focuses on the most extreme contrast: Helsinki and Dublin.

Figure 1. Normal mode of travel to work for employed car owners in six Dublin and Helsinki districts, 1999

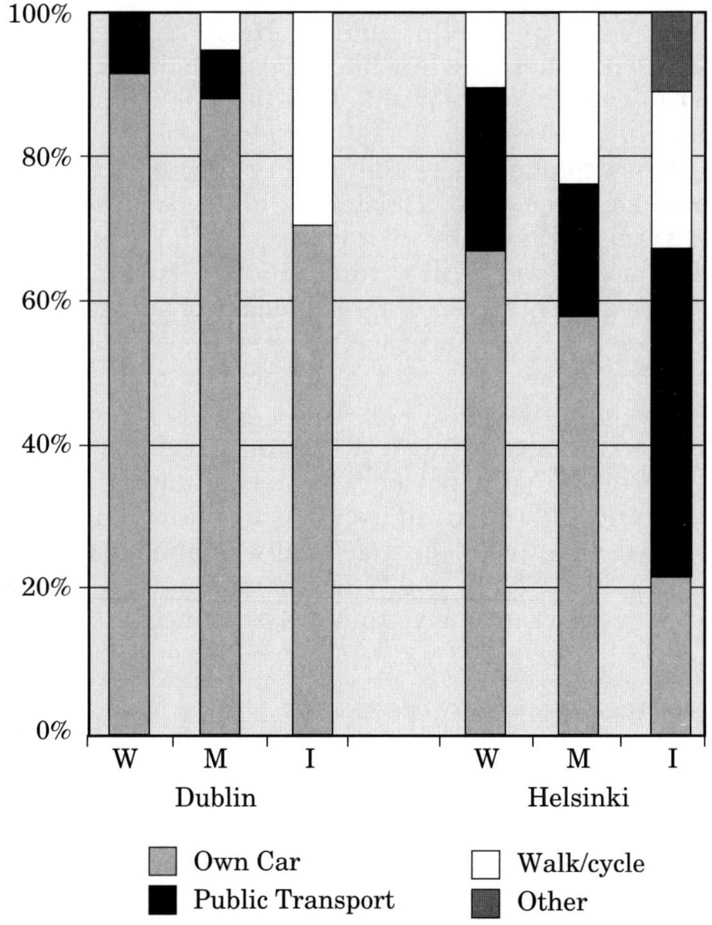

Base: All car owners aged 25 to 64 years who are employed.

Figure 1 shows that in the two Dublin suburban areas, car owners are more likely to use their cars than in any of the other four areas. The middle-class suburbs of Helsinki (Länsi-Pakila) and Dublin (Clonskeagh) used in the survey are both low density and affluent areas: they comprise single-family houses inhabited largely by families with children and with at least one car per household. Yet comparing the local data, whether from the ethnography, the survey or the focus groups, shows clear contrasts. Figure 1 shows higher levels of car usage for travel to work in Dublin than in Helsinki. In suburban Helsinki, car owners are less likely to use their cars than car owners in Dublin and more likely to use public transport or bicycles.

The key explanation is the quality of public transport. Compared to a city like Helsinki, Dublin does not have a public transport system in any meaningful sense of the words: there is very little integration between different routes, let alone between different modes of transport, even though nearly all the transport is provided by state-owned companies. Unlike cities with good public transport, there is no single organisation overseeing public transport in Dublin, and there certainly is no urban or regional authority with any meaningful power.[5] In this situation transport decisions are made on an ad hoc basis by national politicians who are not directly responsible to any Dublin electorate. At best, a city like Dublin gets a few prestige projects; it does not get a system responsive to its citizens' needs.

Car dependency and social exclusion

The corollary of poor public transport is car dependency, where people use cars because they have no choice of any alternative mode of transport. In a car-dependent city it is essential to own a car (or at least have access to one) in

5 There is a Dublin Regional Authority, comprising representatives of the Dublin area councils, but its powers are limited.

order to participate in normal activities – not just employment, but shopping, socialising etc.

This can clearly be seen by contrasting the two Northern European suburban working-class areas in our study: Jobstown (Tallaght) in Dublin and Kontula in Helsinki. Both were built as public housing for a low-income population; Kontula was constructed in the late 1960s, Jobstown in the late 1980s. Kontula comprises large concrete apartment blocks; Jobstown by contrast is low-rise terraced housing. Their building styles and their peripheral locations are typical of post-World War II working-class housing in their respective countries;[6] they are both areas of high unemployment. What happens when areas designed in this way are inhabited by people for whom owning a car is often difficult and sometimes impossible?

The most obvious form of exclusion is from employment. Without a car, access to jobs is limited in Dublin, but not in Helsinki. Car ownership in both Kontula and Jobstown is very low in comparison to almost all other areas in the study, with only about 50 per cent of the households owning a car. Nonetheless, Figure 1 shows that Jobstown has the highest level of car use for the journey to work of all six areas, revealing the vital importance of using a car to get to work. As one focus group[7] participant remarked:

> Well we have always had a car, of one description or another, since we moved to Jobstown but I used to say so often that it was the biggest drain on our finances ... We could live comfortably if we didn't have this car. And we had to have it, to live. And there was no alternative for

6 A. Power, *Estates on the Edge: The Social Consequences of Mass Housing in Northern Europe*, London: Macmillan, 1998.

7 For full accounts of the focus groups see Taina Rajanti (ed.), *Experiencing Mobility, Imagining Accessibility: Results from Focus Groups in Four European Cities*, Dublin: Employment Research Centre, Trinity College Dublin, 2002 (www.tcd.ie/erc/cars). The Dublin report was compiled by Maria Lohan, and the Helsinki report by Taina Rajanti.

> him to get to work other than if he left the house at 6 o'clock in the morning to go all the way into town to come back out again to Lucan. Yet, if he had a car, he could go across that road in 15 to 20 minutes.

This is particularly important for people whose workplaces are the new factories and distribution centres along the M50 orbital motorway. Conversely, those who do not have a car can only reach a much narrower range of jobs.

Given the lack of public transport, reaching the city centre is time-consuming for many of the inhabitants of Jobstown. Indeed, if there are other commitments in the day it is effectively impossible because the bus service is unreliable. One focus group participant explains why she cannot go into the city once she has left her young child at school:

> I could go into town right in the morning after leaving him off, and if I was lucky it would take three-quarters of an hour once I'd be on the bus. But if I was unlucky, it could take me an hour and a half or more, so I'd never be sure that I'd be out again by 12.30 to collect him. And so I can't do that [go to the city centre during the week] because I have to be there for him.

The contrast with Kontula, which has a large shopping centre and a metro station, is dramatic. Certainly this is no tourist attraction: the metro station is just about clean, it is bare and functional, and there is some graffiti. Nonetheless, the area as a whole is well served by buses and in addition there is a so-called 'service-line' or smaller internal bus-line. Everybody lives within 500 metres of a bus stop, most within 250 metres. One metro stop away is Itäkeskus, a huge shopping-cum-service centre, with all the main department stores and also all public facilities. And Kontula is only 17 minutes away from Helsinki city centre by metro.

This easy mobility was highlighted by the survey, which asked non-car owners what they would gain by having a car. In Jobstown, 33 per cent mentioned access to employment, as against only 4 per cent in Kontula. More generally, whereas in Kontula only 11 per cent of non-car owners felt that a car was an absolute necessity for them, in Jobstown the proportion was 63 per cent. Equally, in Kontula fully one-third of the respondents were adamant they would not buy a car, even if they had the money – an option chosen by nobody in Jobstown. When those who did own a car in Kontula were asked in a focus group what impact drastic restrictions on car usage would have for them, they could imagine little major change in their daily lives.

The contrast between Kontula and Jobstown suggests that citizens of Dublin, unlike citizens of Helsinki, find it difficult to move around their city unless they have a car. They lack access to public spaces, whether of the 'parochial' or in particular the 'public' sort. In this sense, citizens of Dublin lack an important element of urban citizenship. Lack of mobility and access is tantamount to social exclusion; it is the denial of one fundamental right of urban citizenship.

Social cohesion

Exclusion is by definition experienced by one section of the population. By contrast, social cohesion, if this is understood as the opposite of Durkheim's anomie, affects everyone. Within an area like Jobstown, many of the inhabitants' problems are caused by other inhabitants. Public transport is 'public' only in the sense of an unpleasant and dangerous space, as another focus group participant remarked:

> I was going to town last week [by bus]. It was 10 in the morning and nobody could use upstairs. A lot of boys had got off at the community centre before 10 and I suppose they had come out from town because the bus was after coming from town and whatever they were at, they had made a public toilet of upstairs.

Such activities are experienced most directly by those who are also excluded. In Dublin, however, even 'middle-class' public transport spaces can be undermined, as recent newspaper reports about threatening behaviour on the DART light railway indicate (*The Irish Times*, 17 February 2003). If public spaces are dangerous, the sensible person avoids them and gets into his or, in particular, her car.

Comparisons between the middle-class suburbs of Helsinki and Dublin suggest that this retreat from the public spaces of mobility is pre-programmed. In Clonskeagh, what strikes one, according to our ethnographic reports, is 'the quietness of it all', whereas in Länsi-Pakila 'there are people walking – kids and adults'. The physical layout of Länsi-Pakila facilitates cycling and walking in a way that Clonskeagh does not. The main roads in Clonskeagh frequently have no cycle lanes or even footpaths, thus discouraging cycling and walking outside the immediate estates, although within the estates there are adequate footpaths and traffic is calmed by speed ramps. In Länsi-Pakila, by contrast, roads around the area, even though busy, have well-kept pedestrian/bicycle lanes, including pedestrian/bicycle gravel lanes which traverse the area almost completely within woods. Even in the Finnish winter many are swept clean and all are in use. Accordingly, in Länsi-Pakila the physical layout facilitates those who wish to walk or cycle, thus creating small-scale public mobility spaces. Whereas in Clonskeagh, despite the milder climate, the car is the only mode of transport that is facilitated.

Not surprisingly, in Länsi-Pakila young people have more what we could term 'mobility skills' than their counterparts in Clonskeagh, not least because they are noticeably more likely to go to school by public transport or by bicycle. The focus groups showed that for many participants in Helsinki learning to use the public transport system is part of their identity as accomplished urban citizens. It is the public transport system that gives them the consciousness that they can move about their city, that they have choices, and hence that, in these terms, they can control their lives through the use of public structures. In Helsinki, unlike

Dublin, some older members of our focus groups linked public transport and public spiritedness. For them, part of the definition of public transport is that it is owned by the 'public' and good citizenship involves a preference for public means.

Conclusion

Clearly Dublin's car dependency is hardly the sole cause of its inhabitants' weak citizenship. Nonetheless, an adequate public transport system is one way in which a city can be tied together. Such a system enables inhabitants of the city to exercise a right to mobility and contributes to social inclusion, making urban citizenship a reality for all who live in the city. However, the right to mobility is only meaningful if the obligation of appropriate behaviour in public places is also enforced; without this, other users will be driven to private transport solutions and public transport will become a system of last resort. To the extent that this decline does not happen, public transport not only makes public spaces accessible, it creates a public space.

In one sense, therefore, public transport creates citizens and public civility. Here there is a reciprocal relationship with public institutions. One reason for Dublin's poor public transport is the lack of a city transit authority and any democratic metropolitan structure of government. This institutional deficit is in turn both cause and effect of the weakness of citizenship. Without strong citizenship, there is little pressure for accountable city government; without an accountable city government, there is little sense of citizenship. Dublin is, therefore, stuck in a vicious circle, and the government's contribution is merely to attempt to privatise a public enterprise like Dublin Bus, thus further narrowing the public realm and reducing the scope for urban citizenship. Perhaps it is not so surprising after all that cows get cut up in Dublin.

CHAPTER 17

Random Attacks?

CIARAN McCULLAGH

As the Republic of Ireland approached the twenty-first century, the situation in relation to its crime levels appeared favourable, with the figures falling consistently since 1996. This was the source of some celebration among the governing coalition parties, who attributed the fall to their policy of zero tolerance. But from 1999 onwards, public attention came to focus on the apparent increase in violent assaults and in related public order offences.

Figures on crimes of violence are notoriously susceptible to reporting problems. Official figures in this area are an unreliable guide to the level of such offences and therefore the precise levels of assault remain unknown and probably unknowable in most societies. Yet this time around in Ireland there was little willingness to dismiss the rise in assaults as a quirk of the methods of reporting and recording crime. Indeed the figures triggered a major debate about crime, led to changes in the policing of city-centre entertainment areas and brought about a reversal in the recently liberalised law on the opening hours of public houses and nightclubs. The major focus of concern was on the apparently random nature of these attacks.

This chapter argues that public concern about these crimes had all the characteristics of a moral panic. That is to say, the nature of the threat that these assaults posed was exaggerated and media coverage was both selective and disproportionate. This created the impression that this kind of crime was extensive and, somewhat more worryingly, pointless, unmotivated and without pattern. In this way the threat was perversely democratised, raising the possibility that everyone was a potential victim. These violent assaults became an issue of major social concern and, given the apparently random nature of the attacks, they came to stand as a symptom of moral and social decline.

However, while there may or may not have been an increase in the number and frequency of such attacks, it will be argued here that the terms in which the problem was presented concealed a significant change in the class relationships that underpin and generate street violence. The frame of reference in which 'random attacks' were discussed in Ireland led to the glossing over of 'the potentially awkward and embarrassing issue of class'.[1] Yet the issue of class may, in a perverse and unexpected way, have been at the heart of this particular 'crime wave'.

A moral panic

The concern about violent assault had its origins in the media, particularly in talk radio. Marian Finucane's popular programme on RTÉ Radio 1, for example, gave considerable coverage to accounts from the mainly male victims, or more commonly from their mothers, of the apparently random attacks that they had suffered in city and town centres. Newspaper reporting tends to complement and reinforce issues discussed on the airwaves. The concern was echoed in the provincial press, which suggested that a similar type of violence was affecting cities and towns as diverse as Sligo, Ennis, Tralee, Roscommon, Longford, New Ross and Wexford. A journalist in Kilkenny, for example, observed

1 J. Best, *Random Violence*, California: University of California Press, 1999, p. 22.

that: 'the number of random attacks in the city does seem to have increased', though she went on to add that, while she did most of her work at night, she had not personally witnessed the violence (*The Irish Times*, 13 June 2001).

Victim Support, an organisation that, as its name suggests, represents the interests of crime victims, further amplified the concern. In a statement issued on 2 August 2000, attention was drawn to a rise in what it termed 'personal, unprovoked attacks' and in particular to the increase in such attacks on young men aged between 17 and 25 years. Victim Support also claimed that in many cases the victims had not reported these offences to the Garda Síochána. The reasons given for this decision included a 'lack of confidence in the gardaí and fear of reprisals'. Initial approaches to Victim Support were not, as one might expect, made by the victims themselves. The reporting had been done by their parents, and generally by their mothers, who were concerned that their sons were not recovering from the trauma of sudden and unexpected assaults.

The public and media attention intensified when an assault resulted in serious injury or death. This was the case in January and February 2002 when, in separate incidents, two young men were attacked in the centre of Cork and left on life-support machines in the local hospital. One subsequently died from his injuries. The attacks in Cork led to a period of sustained attention by the local media to street violence in the city, and in particular by the local evening newspaper, the *Evening Echo*.

The level of concern provoked by the issue appeared to be justified by the release in January 2002 of the crime figures for 2000. These showed a 131 per cent increase in the number of reported violent assaults between 1999 and 2000. By any standards this was a significant increase. Taken together with the proposition that many of these assaults were random and unprovoked, it appeared that a social change of some significance was occurring. But was it that simple, and, if we are talking about significant change, what was the nature of that change?

It is difficult to decipher the crime picture from the media, as its coverage had many of the features that sociologists associate with a moral panic, most notably the exaggerated and disproportionate reporting of certain kinds of crime. A study of the coverage of the attacks in Cork city by the *Evening Echo* confirms the distorted nature of crime coverage.[2] Such coverage can only have increased concern and anxiety in the city. In the initial aftermath of the attack that left one young man dead, the newspaper gave extensive coverage to the issue of crime. This included the coverage of a conference on crime organised by local Fine Gael TD, Simon Coveney, in which prominence was given to the call from a former judge for the closing of all nightclubs in the city on the grounds that they were 'places of evil'. The *Echo* also reported that a representative of the Small Firms Association in the city called for an end to syringe attacks, despite the fact that these had been declining at national level since 1996 and had never been a problem in the city anyway.

The *Echo* also ran a series of articles with headlines such as 'Fear and loathing on the streets of Cork' (6 February 2002) and 'Why walking the streets of Cork is no longer safe' (11 February 2002). The concern with attacks on young men soon expanded to include the old reliable in terms of crime reporting: attacks on older people. It was reported that 'Cork elderly citizens say they are afraid to live in their own homes and answer their front doors' (6 February 2002). Figures from the local hospital were also highlighted as they showed an increase in the number of people being admitted as a result of personal violence. Yet material in the articles belied the tone of the headlines. The problem with older people was said 'not to be widespread' (6 February 2002), while the figures for the hospital referred only to those that 'claimed to be assaulted' (11 February 2002). These important qualifications were capable of an equal level of

2 E. Keating, 'Moral Panics and Street Disorder', BA student thesis, University College Cork, 2003.

attention from the newspaper, but did not receive it. The newspaper also invited comments from victims of street crime as it wanted to give a platform to their views. As the newspaper never followed this up, one can only assume that no-one came forward or that anyone who did was unwilling or unable to substantiate his or her case.

Media coverage also led to routine events being presented as new and as responses to the initial problem when they were not. Thus, on 6 March 2002, the *Echo* reported that the Garda Commissioner was coming to Cork 'in response to a public outcry after recent brutal assaults'. The newspaper told its readers that 'A top-level law and order summit will be held in Cork next week by Garda boss Pat Byrne after recent street attacks'. However the meeting was part of a series of visits that the commissioner had been making to regional divisions. It would have happened whether the violent incidents had occurred or not. Similarly, the newspaper reported that 'public pressure has been mounting for a greater Garda presence on the streets' and it was being responded to through Operation Encounter. On closer examination, this initiative appears to have been simply a rebranding of a pre-existing programme, Operation Óiche.

The halo effect

Newspaper coverage also embodied important aspects of the 'halo effect' that commentators have noted in moral panics. Once panics start over specific types of incidents, other unrelated ones get drawn into the media coverage and are presented as if they were supporting evidence for the underlying thesis. So newspaper articles dealing with the issue were often illustrated with examples of violent incidents that did not quite fit the image of pointless and random violence. For example, an article in *The Irish Times* on 23 August 2000 detailing the response of Victim Support to random, unprovoked attacks concluded with accounts of two violent incidents, one on a 73-year-old woman and the other on a German student. While certainly unprovoked, these were not entirely random or unmotivated attacks, as robbery appears to have been the purpose in both cases.

Elements of a moral panic are also evident in the way in which the media dealt with contrary information. The media did not always ignore information that might have questioned the scale of the problem, but it did present the information in a way that undermined its credibility or dismissed its relevance. So the media did allude to the possibility that there could be a problem with the way in which crime statistics were gathered, most notably the move within the Garda Síochána from a system that was manual to one that was computerised. This, it was reported in *The Irish Times* on 18 February 2002, was likely to lead to an increase of up to 1,000 per cent in the number of recorded assaults, as under the old system it was 'normal practice only to record those assaults which were of a serious nature. Now every reported assault is recorded'. However, the report went on to say: 'no matter what accounting system is used, Gardaí *appear to agree* that late-night street violence is increasing' (italics added). The reporter also noted that a senior garda officer had told him that experienced gardaí were 'now expressing concern that some town centres were becoming too dangerous to police'.

A suitable culprit

Further evidence of a moral panic can be found in the way in which the media honed in on a suitable culprit to explain the crime wave. Official explanations for the violence pointed to the central role of alcohol. This was supported by the claim that alcohol consumption had increased by 41 per cent between 1989 and 1999. The then Garda Commissioner concluded that 'the aggressiveness in young and not so young people' was caused by alcohol. This was the drug with which he had the greatest problems (*The Irish Times*, 22 February 2002). The then Minister for Justice said that 'State agencies cannot solve the problems associated with excessive drinking'. 'Society', he went on, 'has a big problem dealing with the lethal combination of excessive drinking and the aggressive machismo of young men'. This was, he said, 'a problem that will never be solved' (*Irish Examiner*, 15 April 2002). In this way alcohol became, in Nils Christie's phrase, 'both a symbol of and a target for all social anxieties'.[3]

This kind of explanation, however, evaded key questions such as why Irish people were drinking so much and why drink was making them violent. Drunkenness and violence on the part of Irish people are not always synonymous. Witness the good-natured and exemplary behaviour of Irish soccer fans attending matches at home and abroad, despite the large quantities of alcohol consumed by some. Their behaviour is generally seen in a positive light, particularly in comparison to their English counterparts.

Symbolic solutions

The notion that Ireland was in the presence of a moral panic was reinforced when the Minister for Justice announced a suitably draconian series of measures to deal with the 'epidemic', thus meeting the requirement that moral panics provoke symbolic solutions. This had the virtue of appearing to be a clear example of tough government action on behalf of the public. On closer examination, it was somewhat less than that. Part of the response involved the presentation of existing laws in a new guise accompanied by an updating of the penalties attached to such offences. It had always, for example, been illegal for publicans to serve customers who were drunk, but the minister presented this as if it was a new feature and attached a more severe penalty to it. He also introduced new powers of arrest for drunkenness, again conveying the impression of decisive action, but the powers

3 N. Christie, 'Suitable enemies', in H. Bianchi and R. van Swaaningen (eds.), *Abolitionism: Towards a Non-Repressive Approach to Crime*, Amsterdam: Free University Press, 1986, p. 50.

were, according to lawyers and civil liberties groups, sufficiently vague as to be unworkable and possibly unconstitutional.

The plan also included a proposal to restrict the opening hours of the pubs and in particular to cut back on late opening on a Thursday night. This subsequently became law, yet it is one of the changes that is particularly open to the accusation of window dressing. An analysis of public order offences has shown that they occur most frequently on Saturday and Sunday mornings.[4] So, logically, the opening hours on Friday and Saturday nights were the ones that should have been restricted. Curtailing them on Thursday had the virtue of appearing to be tough while avoiding the kind of head-on collision with a politically powerful group like publicans that earlier closing on weekends would have involved.[5]

A new dimension of street crime

It is clear then that institutional responses to the increase in violent crime statistics had significant elements of the over-reaction that is characteristic of moral panics. However, it is not enough to leave it at that. This would be to ignore the extent to which something new was going on and also to misunderstand the role that moral panics play in contemporary Irish society. Moral panics have moved from being the means through which the normative boundaries of society are re-asserted to a means used by social groups to draw attention to new issues and to get them onto the media

4 National Crime Council, *Public Order Offences in Ireland*, Dublin: Government Publications, 2003.

5 This change was sweetened by a very significant concession to publicans: cases of discrimination against Travellers will no longer be heard by the Equality Authority; instead, they will be heard in the District Court – a change that publicans had been pursuing for some time as they believe that they will lose less of these cases there.

and political agendas.[6] And I suggest that the issue struggling to find a voice here was not that the attacks were random and unmotivated, but the fact that they were not. What was new was that many of the assaults were committed by young working-class men on middle-class victims, mostly third-level students. Contrary to the 'normal' pattern of street violence, these attacks crossed class lines. Increasingly, young middle-class men were becoming the victims of their working-class counterparts.

A full substantiation of this argument would require a level of empirical detail that is currently not available, most notably an analysis of the social backgrounds of victims and offenders. However, this kind of information is not routinely collected in court records and many of the more high profile cases are not open to analysis as the courts have yet to adjudicate on them. Yet there are a number of indicators of the role that class played in the panic. These can be considered to be examples of the way in which suppressed issues find their way out of the social subconscious and into the public arena. Their meaning does not have to be explicitly articulated, but can be 'read' by that section of the audience to whom they are addressed. The examples below are drawn again from the coverage of the *Evening Echo* newspaper.

In the middle of February 2002, the *Echo* ran a week-long investigation into street violence. To give the reports instant recognition within the newspaper, they were accompanied by a logo of a young man with his clenched fist prominently displayed in, as it were, the face of the reader. The day that the attack on a student was reported, this logo was subtly altered. The image of the young man was superimposed on a map of the area in which this particular attack had happened. But more significantly the figure in the logo was now wearing a 'hoodie'. This item of clothing has a

6 S. Watney, *Policing Desire: Pornography, AIDS, and the Media*, London: Cassell, 1997, 3rd edn.

particular connotation for some in the city and indeed nationally: it symbolises dangerous working-class youths.

On 23 February 2002, the *Echo* interviewed a student who had been the victim of a random assault. Two days later it gave considerable coverage, by tabloid standards, to a report on a proposed safety programme aimed at students. This was given two paragraphs and a large headline. The programme, it said, would be up and running 'in a few weeks'. The previous night a young man had been attacked and stabbed in Knocknaheeny, a working-class estate in the city. The attack had been sufficiently serious to put him into intensive care. Yet the attack only merited a small headline, less text and no photograph in the same edition of the *Echo*.

On 5 March, a report in the *Echo* warned young people of 'no-go' areas to avoid in the city. Again you might anticipate that this advice would have been aimed at all young people, but it was not. The comments were from a student leader and were directed to a student audience. On 8 March, the *Echo* gave prominence to a local politician calling for the setting up of a scheme to enable young people to get taxis home at night when they had run out of money. If the concern was about all victims of violence this scheme would have been aimed at all young people, but once again it was not. The politician asked third-level institutions in Cork to set up and underwrite the scheme with local taxi companies.

Crossing the class divide

While these examples are not empirically decisive, they are sufficiently striking to suggest that we are witnessing a new phenomenon in terms of violence in Ireland. The moral panic detailed here may not simply have been about violence as such. It may also have been about violence that crossed the class divide. This is evident in the disproportionate coverage given to student fears of crime, to student victims of street assault and to student responses to the issue – to the exclusion of concern with the more 'traditional' victims of violence: young working-class males. These attacks may not have been random. A significant number of the assaults may have been attacks on the most visible manifestation of middle-class status to young people, that of the student, by young working-class and socially excluded males.

If the attacks were not random, it is also possible that they may, at a very crude level, have been motivated. We are not helped in understanding this by conventional criminology, which sees the motivation for assault as arising in the context of 'male honour contests'. In many cases, Levi argues, assaults are the result of 'an escalating interactive process' between two people, generally men.[7] They begin with accidental jostling or a wrongly interpreted look and escalate into a major honour contest. Conventional criminologists also argue that street violence is often misrepresented in the media as involving an innocent victim and a guilty offender. The 'normal kind of assault', Levi tells us, 'is one among people who have some prior acquaintance'.[8] As a result, the 'normal' victim of street violence is as likely as the perpetrator to have a criminal record. It also tends to be intra-class in nature, involving working-class offenders and victims.

But it is possible that the motivations in street violence and the relationships between victims and offenders are more complex than this analysis allows. In the Cork situation outlined above, it is possible that there may be elements of class anger and class resentment behind the street attacks. The victims may have been assaulted not for who they are but for what they represent: figures of privilege in a class-divided society. Students may have become the momentary focus for the incoherent anger that has been produced in some young working-class men by the unequal attentions of the Celtic Tiger and its resulting affluence.

7 M. Levi, 'Violent Crime', in M. Maguire (ed.), *Oxford Handbook of Criminology*, Oxford: Oxford University Press, 1998, p. 843.
8 ibid., p. 842.

CHAPTER 18

Reclaiming the Streets

JOE MOFFATT

Thousands and thousands of people have, over the years, participated in protests in their communities, towns and cities: the unemployed, workers, farmers, students, pupils and parents, environmentalists, republicans, local residents, cultural minorities etc. The issues at the heart of such protests have also been varied: anti-racism, anti-globalisation, anti-war, anti-water charges, anti-bin tax, anti-drugs, anti-hospital closures etc. Practically none of these events have been characterised by violence. Protest rallies and marches in the Republic of Ireland tend to be rather peaceful affairs. It is highly unusual to hear that people have been arrested at any protest or that any form of violence has taken place, be it from protestors or police. Reclaim The Streets gatherings in the past, although not authorised, have passed without incident. However, the Street Party organised on May Day 2002 by Reclaim The Streets was marred by violence and arrests.

The May Day event was widely advertised through graffiti, flyers, posters and word of mouth, and a large turnout was expected. Approximately 400 people left the meeting point at the GPO at around 2.30pm. Their numbers had swelled to between 600 and 800 by 3pm, when the group reached the site for the Street Party at Burgh Quay. People spread out onto the road to stop cars from passing: this closed the quay to motorised traffic. Sound systems were produced and a samba band performed. The quay was colourfully decorated with flags and banners, and people danced, talked and played games for the next few hours. It is estimated that over one thousand people were in attendance at the height of the gathering.

A confrontation occurred on Burgh Quay at around 4pm when, in a symbolic act directed at the dominant car culture, a derelict car made available by Reclaim The Streets activists was smoke bombed. Arrests were made as some activists pushed the car into a safe position, away from the Street Party, for the ritual smoke bombing. By 6.30pm the revellers had decreased in numbers to between 200 and 250 people. A decision was made that the group would make its way to St Stephen's Green and then disperse. However, as it made its way up Dame Street, blocking traffic as it progressed, the police attacked.

The attack on the Reclaim The Streets event was well documented and publicised, but no explanation has been offered to account for it. This chapter is an attempt to explain the action of some gardaí on that day, an explanation which revolves around the concept of deviance amplification.

Deviance amplification

Behaviour that fails to conform to commonly agreed norms, values and beliefs is frequently labelled as deviant. The concept of deviance amplification was coined and developed by L. T. Wilkins.[1] Why are certain acts or attitudes tolerated in some cultures and not in others, and why is it that an accommodation toward deviance may in some cultures prevent the development of more serious acts of deviance?

[1] L. T. Wilkins, 'The Deviance-Amplifying System', in W. G. Carson and P. Wiles (eds.), *Crime and Delinquency in Britain*, London: Martin Robertson and Company, 1971.

The theory of deviance amplification suggests that what is considered socially deviant often constitutes the accidental outcome of a moral panic. When an activity or group has been labelled deviant, or measures are taken to address the deviance, this can lead to a perceived increase in the level of deviance in society. In elaborating the theory, Wilkins relied on the example of illegal drug usage in Britain and the US.

In the 1960s, it was felt that drug misuse in Britain did not indicate a 'real problem', while in the US it represented a 'very considerable problem',[2] even though both countries would have had similar or comparable experiences of drug usage. Wilkins stressed several factors that explain this difference, but she emphasised particularly the role of perceptions: how drug addicts are perceived, how the police view matters, how crime is comprehended. For example, if drunken public disorder came to be considered a serious problem in Ireland and gardaí were to adopt an attitude of zero tolerance towards such displays of public disorder – detaining people for jaywalking, causing a public nuisance, drinking on the street etc. – thousands of people would be arrested on any given weekend throughout the country. Those many thousands of people would then pass through the courts each year, leading observers to conclude that drunken public disorder had massively increased. In other words, this type of deviance would have been amplified.

The concept of deviance amplification applies to the May Day 2002 event and accounts, at least in part, for the violent response of gardaí to the gathering. It is argued in this chapter that the deviant character of the Reclaim The Streets protest was considerably amplified by a range of factors and mechanisms: the profile of the participants, the nature of the protest, the ideological frame of the police and the media's linking of the event to a number of high profile anti-globalisation protests.

2 ibid., p. 258.

Reclaim The Streets

Reclaim The Streets (RTS) could be considered representative of a new social movement. Its political orientation is radical: humanist and ecological, it calls for dramatically improved public transport facilities along with expanding and integrated public spaces. RTS was formed in London in 1991 with the intention of highlighting the ecological and social damage brought about by mass car usage:

> Cars dominate our cities, polluting, congesting and dividing communities. They have isolated people from one another, and our streets have become mere conduits for motor vehicles to hurtle through, oblivious of the neighbourhoods they are disrupting. Cars have created social voids; allowing people to move further and further away from their homes, dispersing and fragmenting daily activities and lives and increasing social anonymity.[3]

The originators of RTS targeted the capitalist socio-economic system and more particularly those that have a vested interest in continuing the promotion of the car: the oil companies, car manufacturers, road constructors and the state. This anti-capitalist sentiment remains a common theme at RTS events in Ireland and globally, as illustrated by the banners carried by participants.

RTS is a transnational, non-authoritarian, ad hoc and non-hierarchical grouping. It has no controlling centre, no leaders or membership lists. There is no commitment or pressure to treat RTS as an ongoing activity and it holds very few meetings. RTS has a loose network of activists, through which people can co-ordinate similar events on the same day in many different cities. But there is absolutely nothing preventing any RTS grouping from establishing itself anywhere. If a group of people is sufficiently concerned about a dominant car culture to take action and show their

[3] http://rts.gn.apc.org/evol.htm

RTS flag © *Workers Solidarity Movement, 2002*

opposition, they may use the label RTS – with its history and philosophy, its downloadable flyers and posters – to publicise an event. This label has proved to be an effective mechanism to highlight such concerns.

Participants in RTS events are typically in their mid-twenties and under. They predominantly come from a range of sub-cultural categories: anti-capitalists, punk rockers, new age travellers, anarchists, environmentalists, artists etc. Most participants share a political attitude that challenges accepted views of what is *the political* in Ireland. RTS mobilises people not for a march or a picket but instead for a Street Party. The prevalent attitude is that direct action brings about social change: people must involve themselves in promoting and directing changes in order to ensure that such changes come to fruition.

The best-known tactic of RTS is the Street Party. This was first used in London in 1995, but has diffused around the globe with regular Street Parties being held in North

America, Australia and Europe. The Street Party is an ideal expression of the RTS philosophy of direct action: it allows people the opportunity to *reclaim the streets* – from cars, from authority, from commercialism – in an atmosphere of carnival and enjoyment. RTS does not *ask* permission from an authority, be it the police or the city council, to hold an event in a public area. It holds an event irrespective of what is authorised, expected or even legal and it maintains a non-co-operative approach with policing and municipal authorities regarding public assembly. This approach makes RTS highly unconventional when compared to other Irish radical groupings like the Irish Anti-War Movement or Globalise Resistance.

Policing involves controlling a situation. How do you control a fluid protest? How do you police something when you have little idea of what will happen, what is planned, or even if anything is planned? Police make use of snatch squads in public order situations, but how can you identify ringleaders when there are none? Though the police knew the assembly point and time for the Street Party on May Day 2002, they did not know the destination(s) of the party. RTS is associated with free expression, which again causes policing problems. One group might attempt to hold a tennis tournament on O'Connell Street, while another group arranges a soccer game on Eden Quay, and yet another group might try and enhance the appearance of Westmoreland Street with the temporary planting of flowers.

The philosophy and values underpinning RTS renders its adherents politically deviant from mainstream Irish society: a radical political grouping composed mainly of young people; an anti-car attitude; an anti-establishment, if not an anti-capitalist, orientation; an approach that encourages people to do things for themselves and challenge laws if necessary. They accumulate in that way the symbols of political deviance, and the latter become amplified, particularly from the point of view of those who have to police them.

The Garda Síochána

The label 'sub-cultural group' refers to people who share common values within a larger cultural setting. The Garda Síochána form one such group, for they share attitudes and values that differ at times from Irish society at large. Ciaran McCullagh presents a list of traits that can be identified in police officers.[4] Though police officers may feel a sense of mission towards public duty, they also display, according to McCullagh, suspicion and aggression towards some members of the public. Research commissioned by the National Crime Council investigating public order in Ireland has highlighted how gardaí generally approach young people in a confrontational manner.[5] There is also, of course, a history of allegations that the gardaí approach, for example, Travellers in a different manner from, say, settled people resident in Blackrock, or that they treat members of Sinn Féin less well than members of Fianna Fáil.

Social conservatism is another trait of the Garda Síochána identified by McCullagh. This social conservatism is linked with a strong identification with the mission of upholding the state against internal subversion:[6] the policing of a radical gathering like RTS acquires in such circumstances a strong political tone. However, it is not only the political composition or orientation of RTS that gardaí might have a problem with, but the fact that it produces a situation of large-scale public disorder.

Another important trait identifiable within the sub-culture of the Garda Síochána could be described as insularity. In October 2001, the Burlington Hotel was the scene of police action similar to that of May Day 2002: police bludgeoning protestors as they sat on the ground. No police

4 C. McCullagh, *Crime in Ireland*, Cork: Cork University Press, 1996.

5 National Crime Council, *Public Order Offences in Ireland*, Dublin: Government Publications, 2003.

6 D. P. J. Walsh, *Irish Police: A Legal and Constitutional Perspective*, Dublin: Round Hall Sweet and Maxwell, 1998.

Gardaí at RTS Street Party © *Workers Solidarity Movement, 2002*

officers, only protestors, were charged with offences on that occasion. The Garda Síochána's internal inquiry into the May Day 2002 incident highlighted once again a strong tendency to close ranks and a culture of non-co-operation regarding the investigation of policing actions. Approximately one hundred and fifty gardaí were involved, throughout the day, in policing the RTS gathering. Twenty-five or so gardaí came voluntarily forward to assist the inquiry, but not one garda identified another garda on duty that day from the video evidence, which clearly shows members of the force engaging in violent acts directed at RTS protestors.

Some of the values that are strongly associated with the Garda Síochána are hardly helpful when policing an event that involves a mobilisation of largely young, politically radical people who question the authority of gardaí and have no or little intention of complying with their requests. The features of such a group affront core police values; the playful public disorder that they create upsets the very ethos of the police force. In both these respects, the deviance of such Street Parties is considerably amplified.

Framing the event

The dominant media representation of the May Day 2002 event suggested RTS was an anti-globalisation gathering. RTÉ's news commentary of the event reported that an anti-globalisation event saw clashes between police and protestors. The *Irish Independent* also labelled the event 'anti-globalisation'. Such coverage associated the RTS event with the media representation of anti-globalisation gatherings, particularly large-scale international assemblies, and their portrayal as what seems to approach a 'violence-fest': gatherings with very little political substance, and characterised by people looting, destroying property or attacking the police.

The commercial media, from where most of us are likely to receive our news, have concentrated on and typically sensationalised minority expressions of violence when covering such international gatherings. The violence-fest representation may have encouraged gardaí to approach the RTS event with expectations of a violent confrontation. The commercial media's coverage of the G8 meeting in Genoa in 2001 largely presented a picture of continuous violent conflict between protestors and the Italian police. It was known that people had travelled from Ireland to attend the violence-fest in Genoa. It was then considered 'probable' that some of the people who travelled there from Ireland would be also involved in violent confrontations at home. The potential deviance of the May Day event was then considerably amplified by the media.

On that basis, some gardaí were bound to approach the gathering strongly expecting the presence of troublemakers: because that is just what happens on anti-globalisation protests, particularly on those that adopt a policy of non-co-operation with the police on routing and protest activities. Gardaí could even point to the amplification of deviance by RTS, as they accepted the deviant – troublemakers – label and then enacted their deviance through a variety of street activities.

What Ireland, and particularly Dublin, had been witnessing, and what the Garda Síochána had to police, in the run up to May Day 2002 was increased 'militant protesting amplification'. This amplification was no longer a matter of perception but could be objectively observed. In September 2001, five people were arrested on European Car Free Day for attempting to close down O'Connell Street to traffic. The following month a protest against public–private partnership at the Burlington Hotel witnessed a police baton charge against protestors involved in a sit-down demonstration. Later that same week, two people were arrested at a demonstration against US foreign policy at the American embassy. In April 2002, two protestors against Israeli policy towards the Palestinians climbed a tree at the Israeli embassy and stayed there for some six days. Therefore, on May Day 2002, approximately one thousand people blocking traffic on a city-centre quay, playing loud music and ignoring police commands, reinforced the sense of deviance amplification for the Garda Síochána.

No car zone © *Workers Solidarity Movement, 2002*

Instead of troublesome protests disappearing or decreasing in frequency, they appeared to be growing. This growth in the number of radical protests – be they in the form of a Street Party or climbing a tree – represents a direct challenge to the Garda Síochána's ability to control public order situations. Gardaí do not rely on specialised control units to ensure public order; they consider 'that public order is a concern of the whole force'.[7] The May Day gathering was a public order situation that met with an over-aggressive policing approach, informed not solely by the Garda Síochána's sub-cultural values, but also by the recent histories of radical gatherings in Dublin.

Conclusion

The violent response of the Garda Síochána to the RTS Street Party in Dublin on May Day 2002 has been made the object of a judicial investigation, and six gardaí have been charged with various offences. However, as mentioned above, violence is rarely used in policing public protests in the Republic of Ireland and it is of some significance to inquire why this particular event, or rather type of event, invoked such a response. It has been contended in this chapter that the RTS gathering has been the object of deviance amplification. A range of mechanisms came into play that intensified the deviant character of such groups in the eyes of the public and, more crucially, of the police. The violent response of the Garda Síochána to this event manifested this amplification, but it also contributed to it. The fact that some gardaí involved in the incident did not wear identification numbers and batoned people around the head – practices to be avoided under Garda Síochána procedures – further reinforced this phenomenon.

This occurrence of police violence must be set in the context of a growing concern about policing in Ireland. Publicly voiced allegations of police brutality and corruption

[7] ibid., p. 159.

only highlight the distance the Garda Síochána will have to travel if it wishes to restore the, admittedly idealised, image of the force presented in 1993 by Gemma Hussey: 'The police force of Ireland is generally highly regarded by the population, behaving with responsibility and observing suitably rigid standards. Good relations exist between the Gardaí and the population in most areas'.[8]

In 2001, Dublin City Council considered introducing legislation leading to the effective criminalisation of non-approved protests. The effort failed. Had Dublin City Council successfully introduced its new bye-laws, RTS would have been required to give four weeks' notice to the Council of the plans for the event and seek advance approval. RTS would have had to obtain insurance protection of €3.8 million – as over 300 people attended – as well as restrict the noise levels from the sound systems, thereby defeating the purpose of a Street Party. The Council's failure to limit public protest on city streets, safeguards those streets for future radical action by RTS and other similarly minded protest groups. In addition, the level of publicity generated by the events of May Day 2002 has probably made the streets a safer place for protesters, as the Garda Síochána may be more considerate when gate crashing the next Street Party!

[8] G. Hussey, *Ireland Today: Anatomy of a Changing State*, Dublin: Townhouse, 1993, p. 133.